All About Child Care and Early Education

A Trainee's Manual for Child Care Professionals

Marilyn Segal

Mary Jean Woika

Jesse Leinfelder

Nova Southeastern University,
Mailman Segal Institute for Early Childhood Studies

PEARSON

Boston   New York   San Francisco
Mexico City   Montreal   Toronto   London   Madrid   Munich   Paris
Hong Kong   Singapore   Tokyo   Cape Town   Sydney

Series Editor: Traci Mueller
Series Editorial Assistant: James P. Neal, III
Marketing Manager: Krista Clark
Production Editor: Annette Joseph
Editorial Production Service: Communicáto, Ltd.
Composition Buyer: Linda Cox
Manufacturing Buyer: Andrew Turso
Electronic Composition: Denise Hoffman
Interior Design: Denise Hoffman
Photo Researcher: Katharine S. Cook
Cover Administrator: Joel Gendron

For related titles and support materials, visit our online catalog at www.ablongman.com.

Between the time website information is gathered and then published, it is not unusual for some sites to have closed. Also, the transcription of URLs can result in typographical errors. The publisher would appreciate notification where these errors occur so that they may be corrected in subsequent editions.

Many of the designations used by manufacturers and sellers to distinguish their products are claimed as trademarks. Where those designations appear in this book and Allyn and Bacon was aware of a trademark claim, the designations have been printed in caps or initial caps.

ISBN 0-205-47781-X

Printed in the United States of America

10 9 8 7 6 5 4 3 2 1   09 08 07 06 05

Permission Credit: The Child Development Associate (CDA) Competency Goals and Functional Areas are reprinted with permission from the Council for Professional Recognition.

Photo Credits: p. 3: Tony Freeman, PhotoEdit; p. 23: Dann Tardif, Corbis/New York; p. 46: T. Lindfors, Lindfors Photography; p. 68: Tony Freeman, PhotoEdit; p. 86: Ellen B. Senisi, ImageWorks; p. 116: Richard Hutchings, PhotoEdit; p. 143: Tom Prettyman, PhotoEdit; p. 165: Nancy Sheehan Photography; p. 188: Ariel Skelley, Corbis/New York; p. 204: David Young-Wolff, PhotoEdit; p. 226: Michael J. Doolittle, Image Works; p. 245: Bill Aron, PhotoEdit; p. 264: Robin Sachs, PhotoEdit.

Contents

Introduction

All About Child Care and Early Education: A Trainee's Manual for Child Care Professionals provides a means for acquiring and demonstrating the knowledge and skills of an effective child care practitioner. The *Trainee's Manual* and its companion textbook, *All About Child Care and Early Education: A Comprehensive Resource for Child Care Professionals*, can be used independently by students who want to proceed at their own rate or used in conjunction with a child care course.

The *Trainee's Manual* contains thirteen chapters organized into six areas, corresponding to the six Competency Goals and thirteen Functional Areas described in the Child Development Associate (CDA) program plan of the Council for Professional Recognition.

How to Use the Trainee's Manual

Part I

Each chapter of Part I in the *Trainee's Manual* is a complete and independent learning area. This means that you can begin with the first chapter if you like or with any chapter of immediate concern.

When you have completed all the chapters of the *Trainee's Manual*, you will have produced a valuable resource and practical guide. Your workbook will contain both a summary of the knowledge you have acquired and an important record of the ideas and activities you have implemented in your child care setting.

The *Trainee's Manual* has been field tested in several locations. It has been used successfully as a CDA training curriculum and as the basis for an in-service curriculum for child care providers working in Head Start programs, public schools, and other early childhood settings.

Each chapter in Part I is organized into these nine components:

1. **Overview, Rationale, and Objectives** This component includes an overview of the Functional Area, a statement of the rationale of the chapter, and a set of objectives. The Overview describes the basic content of the chapter. The Rationale relates the content to your role as a child care practitioner. The Objectives identify the set of competencies you will acquire and be able to demonstrate upon completion of the chapter.

2. **Pretest** The Pretest is a tool for determining the extent of your knowledge before completing the chapter content. The answer to each question will be discussed, if you are enrolled in a class.

3. **Self-Assessment** The Self-Assessment component provides the opportunity for you to think about your understanding and skills before completing the training provided in the chapter.

4. **Pretraining Personal Goal** This component directs you to concentrate on topics of importance to you by stating a personal goal and developing an action plan before completing the training.

5. **Objectives** Each objective in the chapter is explained using a variety of materials and illustrations. Completing the fill-in sections will help you think about and expand on the what you have read about each objective.

6. **Observation Opportunities** One or more Observation Opportunities direct your focus to particular areas of each chapter. Each of these exercises asks you to observe children and caregivers, evaluate what you observed, and reflect on your own practices.

7. **Challenge Activities** Each Challenge Activity provides you with an opportunity to demonstrate your competence within an early childhood setting.

8. **Post-Training Wrap-Up** This component helps you integrate your learning in each Functional Area. Having completed the chapter, you are asked to reflect on the training by describing how you reached your personal goal and how you changed your behavior based on the training.

9. **Professional Resource File** At the end of each chapter, you are directed to complete the appropriate assignments to compile a Professional Resource File for that Functional Area.

Part II

Part II of the *Trainee's Manual* is called Preparing the CDA Professional Resource File. It provides guidelines to assist you in two areas: (1) collecting the 17 required items for the Professional Resource Files and (2) writing the Competency Goal Statements on the model developed by the CDA Council for Professional Recognition, as required for national CDA credentialing.

The national CDA is awarded by the Council. Call 800-424-4310 for a complete description of the national CDA assessment process.

The CDA Competency Goals

Chapter 1

Safe

Overview

Safety involves the prevention of injuries to children and to adults.

Rationale

The old adage "Safety first" is especially true for those who are responsible for young children. Young children depend on adults to keep them safe; they do not yet have the knowledge, skills, or judgment to keep themselves out of danger. Therefore, it is the teacher's responsibility to create and maintain a safe environment while also helping children to learn safety skills.

Although as jobs go, caring for young children is relatively safe, teachers do need to be conscious of their own safety needs as well as the children's. Even a minor accident—such as a wrenched back or twisted ankle—can prevent a teacher from doing her job.

Objectives

• *Objective 1*   To learn how to plan safe activities by taking into account children's developmental levels and likely behaviors

• *Objective 2*   To learn how to create and maintain safe classroom and playground environments

• *Objective 3*   To review what to do in case of a medical emergency

• *Objective 4*   To learn safe practices for taking children on field trips

• *Objective 5*   To develop and model good safety habits

• *Objective 6*   To learn how to involve preschool children in developing safety rules for their classroom

• *Objective 7*   To learn how to develop a safety curriculum

• *Objective 8*   To learn how to set up a safe environment for children with special needs

SAFE • Pretest

For each of the following items, circle the most appropriate statement, keeping in mind the rules and regulations for child care centers in your area.

1. Exit signs must be posted:
   a. on at least two doors in every classroom.
   b. on all available exits within the classroom.
   c. above every door in the classroom.

2. The fire evacuation plan must be:
   a. on file in every classroom.
   b. posted in a conspicuous and predesignated place in every classroom.
   c. posted on every available exit.

3. Every adult working in a child care center should know the following number (or numbers) by heart:
   a. the telephone number of every child in the school.
   b. the telephone numbers of the police, the fire department, and the local hospital.
   c. 911.

4. Fire drills must be held:
   a. monthly.
   b. weekly.
   c. yearly.

5. Infant rooms should have:
   a. room dividers.
   b. floor fans.
   c. protected floor space.

6. Electrical outlets:
   a. are not allowed in a preschool.
   b. must be properly covered when not in use.
   c. must be above children's reach or behind heavy equipment.

7. First aid materials must be:

   a. within reach of every child.

   b. in a place in the classroom that is accessible to adults only.

   c. in a locked drawer or file cabinet where the children cannot get them.

For each of the following statements, write an "S" if the practice is a safe practice and a "U" if it is an unsafe practice.

_____ 8. In order to make sure that all the children stay in the classroom, the teacher blocked the second door to make sure only one door could be exited from.

_____ 9. The teacher has placed a sign on the climbing structure on the playground that reads "For 4- and 5-year-old children only."

_____ 10. The director will not let teachers use electric frying pans in the preschool classrooms.

SAFE • Self-Assessment

Indicate how you feel about your skills and abilities in each of the following categories by checking the appropriate column.

	Pretraining		
	Strong	**Satisfactory**	***Needs Improvement***
I can plan safe activities by taking into account children's developmental levels and likely behaviors.	☐	☐	☐
I can create and maintain safe classroom and playground environments.	☐	☐	☐
I know what to do in case of a medical emergency.	☐	☐	☐
I know safe practices for taking children on field trips.	☐	☐	☐
I know how to develop and model good safety habits.	☐	☐	☐
I know how to involve preschool children in developing safety rules for their classroom.	☐	☐	☐
I know how to develop a safety curriculum.	☐	☐	☐
I can set up a safe environment for children with special needs.	☐	☐	☐

SAFE • Pretraining Personal Goal

Based on your pretraining self-assessment, write a personal goal for this Functional Area and an action plan describing how you will accomplish the goal.

Goal _____

_____

_____

_____

Action Plan _____

_____

_____

_____

_____

_____

_____

_____

_____

_____

_____

_____

Save your goal and action plan for the end of this unit so you will be able to answer these questions: How did you accomplish your goal? And how has your behavior changed based on your training?

To learn how to plan activities by taking into account children's developmental levels and likely behaviors

Ms. Better-Safe-Than-Sorry, the director of Trust-Us-with-Your-Children Child Care Center, was reviewing her teachers' daily lesson plans. Her goal was to place a check beside each of the suggested activities that was age appropriate.

Help Ms. Better-Safe-Than-Sorry complete her task by checking off those activities that you feel are age appropriate.

Infant Teacher

☐ Blow up balloons that the infants can play with.

☐ Fill a bin with beans to give the babies a sensory experience.

Toddler Teacher

☐ Have a relay race on the playground.

☐ Play Ring around the Rosy during circle time.

Teacher for Three-Year-Olds

☐ Play Duck-Duck-Goose on the playground.

☐ Play musical chairs in the classroom.

Teacher for Four-Year-Olds

☐ Invite a parent who is a veterinarian to talk to the class about what veterinarians do.

☐ Put out props in the pretend play area in the classroom that will encourage the children to pretend they are veterinarians.

Now, explain what is wrong with any item that you have not checked off.

_____

_____

_____

_____

_____

Helping Children Learn Safe Practices

Keeping children safe involves helping them learn safe practices and safe ways of using equipment. Children learn about safety rules while they are engaged in activities.

At circle time, Mr. Careful solemnly told his 2-year-olds the rules for playing outside on the slide, swings, and scooting toys. Later, on the playground, he was upset when a child ran into a moving swing and another went down the slide on her stomach. "Don't you remember the rules I told you?" he asked.

Explain to Mr. Careful why the children didn't remember the rules.

_____

_____

_____

To learn how to create and maintain safe classroom and playground environments

Mrs. Bruce was the owner of a child care franchise. At a child care convention, she boasted about the fact that all six of her centers were licensed to operate. "I never have any trouble with inspectors," she announced. "You just have to know how to get around them."

Despite Mrs. Bruce's boast, she was not always successful at "getting around" inspectors. A local newspaper writer who was interested in child care standards visited all her centers, pretending to be a parent. Here are some of the things she found:

Beneath each item, list the type of accident that it might cause.

An old crib with widely spaced slats

_____

Electrical outlets that were uncovered

_____

A very heavy door, without a closer, leading to the outside

_____

Sharp table corners

_____

An active play center in front of a large window

_____

An electric fan in the middle of the floor

_____

A bulletin board with push pins

_____

A supply shelf with balloons and plastic bags

_____

A philodendron plant on the table

_____

Wobbly tables

_____

Small, loose rugs

_____

An umbrella in the dress-up area

_____

An outdoor climbing structure made for elementary school children

_____

Scooting toys and trikes without an indication of a direction to ride

_____

Think about the indoor and outdoor environments at your center and mentally inspect them for safety hazards.

What type of accident is least likely to occur in your classroom?

_____

_____

What sort of accident is most likely to occur in your classroom?

_____

_____

How can you prevent it from happening?

_____

_____

What sort of accident is most likely to occur on your playground?

_____

_____

How can you prevent it from happening?

_____

_____

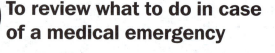

Objective 3
To review what to do in case of a medical emergency

Emergencies are never planned. The time to get ready for an emergency is before it happens.

After each incident description, write a sentence describing how the incident could have been prevented.

A toddler fell out of her highchair while the two caregivers were feeding the younger babies.

_____

Susie fell and cut her knee. Mrs. All-Thumbs went to get a bandage, but the first aid kit had nothing in it but gauze, scissors, and one used rubber glove.

_____

Roberta had a seizure in the classroom. Mrs. All-Thumbs called 911 and explained that the center was on 14th Street across from the hardware store. The paramedics had trouble finding the center.

_____

Pedro was taken to the emergency room by his mother because he had severe stomach cramps. The emergency doctor suggested that Pedro may have eaten the berries from one of the plants on the playground.

_____

Suppose that a child has fallen and may have broken a leg. Fill in each step with the appropriate procedure.

Step 1: Summon help by:

_____

_____

Step 2: Make the child comfortable by:

_____

_____

Step 3: Call the child's parents. If they are not at home or work, call them at their emergency number, which is located on:

_____

_____

Step 4: Follow the procedure for reporting an accident in your center, which is:

_____

_____

To learn safe practices for taking children on field trips

The director of Safety First Child Care Center gave all her caregivers a set of guidelines for taking children on field trips. Add three important guidelines that she forgot to include.

1. Make sure that each child has written permission from a parent or guardian before you take her on a field trip.

2. Arrange for safe transportation to and from the field trip site.

3. Count the children before they leave the center and when they leave the field trip site.

4. Never leave the field trip site unless all the children have been accounted for.

5. _____

6. _____

7. _____

Mrs. Cut-Corners was describing her solution to the transportation problem: "Safe transportation is no problem in our school. Two of our teachers have their own vans. You know, Betsy, the cute 16-year-old? Well, she just got her license and she takes the family van. We can fit 15 kids inside that bugger. Eight kids sit on the floor in the back where it's safe. Six kids sit in the middle, two to a seatbelt, and the baby sits in front on the assistant teacher's lap. I don't let them turn on the motor until the assistant teacher does up her seat belt. 'Safety first' is my motto."

Mrs. Cut-Corners needs your help. Give five reasons her transportation solution is unsafe.

1. _____

2. _____

3. _____

4. _____

5. _____

To develop and model good safety habits

Safety begins by looking in the mirror. If you do dangerous things and at the same time tell the children not to do them, the children will do what you do and pay no attention to what you say. Remember, children learn best by example, and the best way to teach safety is to set a good example.

List three situations in which you saw a teacher doing something dangerous in front of the children.

1. _____

2. _____

3. _____

To learn how to involve preschool children in developing safety rules for their classroom

Both a classroom that is controlled too rigidly and a classroom that is controlled too loosely are at risk for accidents. If a classroom is always "under the teacher's thumb" and the children aren't allowed to do anything unless they are told, then the children do not learn to think for themselves and do not have a chance to learn self-control or develop their own safety standards. In such a class, if the teacher turns away for even a brief period, the children can get rowdy and out of control. A rowdy classroom can be the cause of an accident.

While too tight control of a classroom is bad, too little control is even worse. Children lack the experience to recognize what things or actions are really dangerous. In a classroom where the teacher does not maintain order, it is easy for children to get hurt.

One way to help children recognize safe practices is to let them help you develop a list of safety rules. You are likely to discover that the safety rules children are most likely to contribute are lists of all the things children should not do. Here are some safety rules that were developed by a group of 4-year-olds:

For each rule that is expressed in a negative way, rewrite the rule so that it is expressed in a positive way.

Stop running around and making noise when the teacher makes the lights go on and off.

_____

Don't leave your toys all over the floor.

_____

Don't kick people, even if you're mad.

_____

No standing behind the swings on the playground.

_____

Don't stuff things up your nose or in your ears!

_____

To learn how to develop a safety curriculum

A good way to implement safe activities in your classroom is to begin by making a list of the safety concepts you would like your children to know. Here are some examples for older toddlers and preschoolers:

- Fire can hurt people and property. Because we do not want to start a fire or get burned, we do not play with matches, we keep away from open fires, and we do not put any papers on the stove.
- Cars and trucks are dangerous. We do not run out in the street. We hold onto an adult's hand when we cross the street. We sit in the car with our seatbelts fastened. We do not bother the driver. We obey the traffic signals.

Now it's your turn. Add three other safety concepts to the list.

1. _____

2. _____

3. _____

Once you have developed your list of safety concepts, your challenge is to think of ways to integrate them into everyday activities. Field trips, fire drills, cooking activities, clean-up times, and playtimes provide opportunities for teaching and reinforcing safety concepts.

List three things children can learn about traffic safety when they go for a walk in the neighborhood.

1. _____

2. _____

3. _____

Objective 8

To learn how to set up a safe environment for children with special needs

Mrs. Know-It-All, the director of We Care about All Kids Preschool Center, was talking to a prospective parent:

Prospective Parent: "Your preschool looks very inviting, but I am concerned about your playground. My daughter loves physical activity, but her coordination is not good at all. I know she would not be able to climb on the big climbing structure that I saw on your playground. What do you have on your playground for children like my daughter, Dorothea, who can't play on the fancy structures like the ones you have on your playground?"

Mrs. Know-It-All: "Oh, that has never been a problem. We often have children with physical handicaps, and we make a special effort to help them enjoy playground time. First, we make sure that no child climbs on our structures or slides down the slide unless she has the skills to use that stuff safely. Second, we always have lots of fun things for children to do if they have physical problems. We let them sit in the sandbox and make sand pies. It helps them with hand/eye coordination. We let them blow bubbles to strengthen their lungs, and we let them sit on the benches and watch the other children climb on the structures. You know, children learn a lot about developing physical skills by watching other children who are well coordinated."

Dorothea's mother thanked Mrs. Know-It-All and went to look for a preschool that could accommodate children with physical challenges.

Describe three appropriate ways in which a preschool could set up a playground and plan for playground activities that would be appropriate for children with physical challenges.

1. _____

2. _____

3. _____

SAFE • Observation Opportunity

Name _____

*Using the following checklist to record your observations, spend
10 minutes watching a group of children playing on the playground.*

Observation	Yes	No	Not Observed	Explanation or Comment
Safety practices are followed with riding and scooting toys.	☐	☐	☐	_____ _____
Children go down the slide one at a time.	☐	☐	☐	_____ _____
Children are supervised by the teacher at all times.	☐	☐	☐	_____ _____
Playground equipment is in good repair.	☐	☐	☐	_____ _____
Children are using all playground equipment safely.	☐	☐	☐	_____ _____
Children are not walking behind the swings.	☐	☐	☐	_____ _____
Children play together cooperatively without fighting, pushing, or hitting.	☐	☐	☐	_____ _____

● SAFE ● Challenge Activities

Name _____

Challenge 1

Complete the following for your setting.

Emergency numbers for the children in my care are located:

_____

The fire evacuation plan is located:

_____

The fire extinguisher is located:

_____

In order to operate it, you:

_____

The procedures we follow in a fire drill are:

_____

Our first aid kit is located:

_____

It contains:

_____

My first aid card expires:

_____

Challenge 2

Create a safety checklist with at least 20 items. This list should be specific to your circumstances, setting, and age group. Use it to check the safety of your work setting. Then come up with an action plan for how to correct these hazards.

As you write each item, state it in a positive manner. Phrase each question so that the appropriate answer is "Yes." For example, "Toys are picked up when not in use." Include on the checklist precautions related to these things:

- Ingesting small items
- Tipping over shelves, chests, or dividers
- Tripping and falling
- Sharp corners or protruding hazards
- Traffic flow
- Fingers getting caught or jammed
- Electrical outlets and appliances
- Lead and other kinds of poisons
- Access to the outdoor
- Burns or fires
- Climbing and falling
- Other items related to the rules and regulations enforced in your area

Checklist Item	Yes	No
1. _____	☐	☐
2. _____	☐	☐
3. _____	☐	☐
4. _____	☐	☐
5. _____	☐	☐
6. _____	☐	☐
7. _____	☐	☐
8. _____	☐	☐
9. _____	☐	☐
10. _____	☐	☐

Checklist Item	**Yes**	**No**
11. _____	☐	☐
12. _____	☐	☐
13. _____	☐	☐
14. _____	☐	☐
15. _____	☐	☐
16. _____	☐	☐
17. _____	☐	☐
18. _____	☐	☐
19. _____	☐	☐
20. _____	☐	☐

Action plan to correct any hazards identified:

_____

_____

_____

_____

_____

_____

_____

_____

_____

_____

_____

_____

_____

_____

SAFE • Post-Training Wrap-Up

After completing this unit, review your personal goal and action plan from the beginning of the unit and describe how you accomplished your goal.

_____

_____

_____

_____

List at least three ways in which you changed your behavior as a result of your training in this Functional Area.

1. _____

2. _____

3. _____

SAFE • Professional Resource File

Resource Items

Collect the items for the Professional Resource File related to this Functional Area (if applicable). Refer to the pages at the back of this *Trainee's Manual* (pp. 281–283) and to the CDA booklet from the Council for Professional Recognition for specific instructions.

Statement of Competence

Write a short essay of 75 to 150 words, listing one or more goals you have for keeping children and families safe and describing the activities you do to achieve these goals. Describe your experiences in your own words. Be concise. Use "I" statements—for example, "I check the playground each day for trash and safety hazards like broken toys."

For additional information about writing your Statement of Competence, refer to the workbook section at the end of this *Trainee's Manual* (pp. 283–312) and to the CDA booklet from the Council for Professional Recognition.

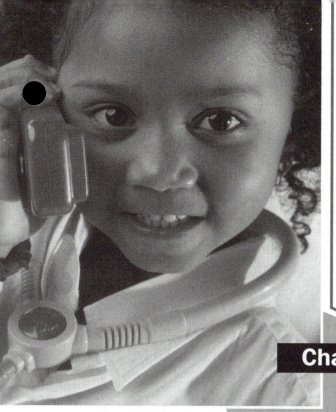

Competency Goal I

To establish and maintain a safe, healthy learning environment

Chapter 2

Healthy

Overview

Often, we think of *health* as simply the absence of disease. It is true that we can't stay healthy unless we learn good health habits that protect our bodies from illness, but we need to think of health in a larger sense. Being healthy means feeling fit and fine. It means having the internal resources to fight off illness and overcome the effects of physical insult; it also means having the energy and stamina to lead a productive life.

Rationale

Health is an important aspect of learning and development. Children who are healthy have the vigor they need to play, learn, and achieve across-the-board development. Also, the more scientists learn about health, the more they become aware of the importance of behavior. Eating right, exercising, avoiding risks, practicing good hygiene and sanitation, and managing stress all contribute to long-term health. The habits acquired in early childhood tend to persist, so it is important to begin early. In addition, nutritional deficits and toxic exposure in early childhood can cause wide-ranging, lifelong problems.

The teacher promotes health within the classroom by doing the following:

- Observing good health practices
- Conforming to health rules and regulations applying to her center
- Recognizing the signs and symptoms of illness
- Developing a program of health education that teaches children to value good health and to follow routines that maintain it

Objectives

● **Objective 1**   To develop a sound knowledge base regarding health, nutrition, and oral hygiene

● **Objective 2**   To carry out routine practices that will prevent illness and promote good health and nutrition

● **Objective 3**   To establish guidelines/policies regarding how to handle health issues, including a record-keeping system

● **Objective 4**   To incorporate activities that teach children and families about health, oral/dental hygiene, and nutrition

● **Objective 5**   To recognize indicators of abuse and/or neglect and follow the reporting policy mandated by the state

● **Objective 6**   To keep oneself healthy and model appropriate wellness behaviors for children and their parents

● HEALTHY ● Pretest

For each of the following, circle the most appropriate statement, keeping in mind the rules and regulations for child care centers in your area.

1. What do you do if a child is ill or has an accident? (Assume that you do not have a school nurse.)
   a. Call the parent.
   b. Call 911.
   c. Either or both of the above, depending on the nature of the illness or accident.

2. What do you do if a child comes down with a communicable disease?
   a. Call the parent and isolate the child.
   b. Call 911.
   c. Send a note home with the child.

3. The primary reason for serving a morning snack is:
   a. that children and their parents have come to expect it.
   b. to avoid midmorning fatigue.
   c. to prevent overeating at lunchtime.

4. A teacher who wants to maximize the health of her children:
   a. reads medical journals.
   b. keeps a good supply of medication on hand for the children.
   c. is aware of the signs and symptoms of childhood illness.

5. *Universal precautions* include which of the following?
   a. Protecting yourself from contact with bodily fluids.
   b. Taking a first aid course.
   c. Wearing disposable gloves when you are with children.
   d. Keeping children safe and healthy when they are in your care.
   e. All of the above

Match each item in the left-hand column to the correct item in the right-hand column.

_____ 1. Chicken pox

_____ 2. Fifths disease

_____ 3. Conjunctivitis

_____ 4. Pin worms

_____ 5. Salmonella

A. Slight fever, blisters appear first on face, back, and under arms

B. Rash, looks as if child was slapped, has a slight fever

C. Diarrhea, flulike symptoms, cramps, vomiting

D. Itching and irritation of anus

E. Red, watery, crusty eyes

Answer True (T) or False (F) to each of the following questions.

_____ 1. Healthy snacks for 2-year-olds include smooth cottage cheese, bananas, rice cakes, and popcorn.

_____ 2. Infants should be put to sleep on their backs.

_____ 3. Always wear disposable gloves when you apply pressure to an open cut.

_____ 4. Healthy food for teeth includes calcium-rich foods like milk and crunchy food like apples.

_____ 5. An infant should never be put to sleep with a bottle in his mouth.

HEALTHY • Self-Assessment

Indicate how you feel about your skills and abilities in each of the following categories by checking the appropriate column.

	Pretraining		
	Strong	*Satisfactory*	*Needs Improvement*
I have a sound knowledge base regarding health, nutrition, and oral hygiene.	☐	☐	☐
I carry out routine practices that will prevent illness and promote good health and nutrition.	☐	☐	☐
I follow guidelines/policies regarding how to handle health issues, including a record-keeping system.	☐	☐	☐
I incorporate activities that teach children and families about health, oral/dental hygiene, and nutrition.	☐	☐	☐
I recognize indicators of abuse and/or neglect and follow the reporting policy mandated by my state.	☐	☐	☐
I keep myself healthy and model appropriate wellness behaviors for children and their parents.	☐	☐	☐

HEALTHY • Pretraining Personal Goal

Based on your pretraining self-assessment, write a personal goal for this Functional Area and an action plan describing how you will accomplish the goal.

Goal _____

_____

_____

_____

Action Plan _____

_____

_____

_____

_____

_____

_____

_____

_____

_____

_____

_____

Save your goal and action plan for the end of this unit so you will be able to answer these questions: How did you accomplish your goal? And how has your behavior changed based on your training?

To develop a sound knowledge base regarding health, nutrition, and oral hygiene

Knowing the Signs and Symptoms of Illness

Mrs. Greene had a conference with Hilary's mother, who had been concerned about Hilary's behavior at home. Before taking her daughter to the clinic, she decided to find out how Hilary was acting at school.

Mrs. Greene: "I am glad that you came to see me. Hilary is such a fine little girl. She is so quiet and good. She never causes any trouble."

Hilary's Mother: "I am happy that you enjoy having Hilary in your class, but I'm concerned about her being as quiet as she is. At home, she seems to have no energy. When she comes home from school, she seems exhausted. She doesn't want to eat dinner, and she just sits around reading books or playing with her dolls. Even on weekends, when I send her out to play in the yard, she appears to tire and run out of breath so much faster than the other children. Have you noticed that at school?"

Mrs. Greene: "Yes, Hilary does get tired on the playground faster than other children. But I wouldn't worry if I were you. You know, all children are different, and Hilary is by nature a quiet and inactive child. I wish all the children in my classroom were just like your Hilary."

Do you agree with Mrs. Greene's last statement? How would you have responded if you were Hilary's mother?

_____

_____

List six signs and symptoms of illness that you feel a classroom teacher should report to a child's parents.

1. _____

2. _____

3. _____

4. _____

5. _____

6. _____

Knowing about Communicable Diseases and Immunization Procedures

Poor Mr. Out-to-Lunch! At the parent/teacher meeting, the parents got on the subject of childhood diseases and immunizations. He was having all kinds of problems with some of the questions.

Use the information found in your textbook in Chapter 2, Health, to help him answer the following questions.

1. My son, Jamie, was exposed to hepatitis A yesterday. If he is going to catch it, when will he start showing symptoms?

    _____

2. My daughter had chicken pox. The rash disappeared two days ago. Can I bring her back to school?

    _____

3. My daughter was sent home with head lice. What am I supposed to do about it?

    _____

4. My son had three DPT shots when he was a baby and one when he was 1½. He won't need more, will he?

    _____

5. Jonathan loved playing with the snake at the child care center. They took it away because one kid got salmonella. Does that make sense?

    _____

6. Tim's friend was playing over at the house yesterday, and his mother told me he woke up with conjunctivitis. Is there any way I can prevent Tim from getting it?

    _____

7. Adam was playing with Theodore on Thursday. Then Saturday morning, Theodore's mother called me to say that Theodore woke up with this rash and the doctor said it was fifths disease. Is there a chance Adam was exposed? He wasn't with Theodore on Friday at all.

    _____

8. I heard a rumor that a child in Brett's infant room has hepatitis B. It's a great child care center, and they are very careful about wearing gloves and washing their hands and all that stuff. But I was still wondering if I should change centers. Should I?

    _____

Sharing Nutrition Information with Families

Jamal, a restless and an active 2½-year-old, opens his lunchbox. As usual, it contains a colored sugar drink and a packaged chocolate cupcake with chocolate icing. When his teacher has tried to talk with his mother about healthy lunches, she has just shrugged her shoulders and said that's the only food Jamal will eat.

Suggest at least two ways that the teacher could help this mother change Jamal's eating habits.

_____

_____

_____

Knowing about Oral Hygiene

Miss Self-Assured was spouting her philosophy about bottle feeding to a new mother: "You know, you don't have to get so uptight about your baby's first teeth. There is absolutely nothing wrong with putting a 1-year-old baby to sleep with a bottle in his mouth. When he's 6 years old, his second teeth will come in, and it won't matter at all if his baby teeth got rotten."

Explain to Miss Self-Assured why putting a baby to sleep with a bottle in his mouth is not a good idea.

_____

_____

2 To carry out routine practices that will prevent illness and promote good health and nutrition

Some of the health routines that you practice in your classroom are dictated by government and licensing agencies. Other routines are a matter of using good judgment and being concerned about the health habits of the children you care for.

Abiding by Health Rules and Regulations

Mrs. Cop-Out was anxious to work with children and hated "all the rigma-role" and "red tape" that was keeping her from doing her job. When her supervisor asked if she knew about the governmental health regulations that applied to her classroom, she got very upset: "It is up to the director, not me, to know about those regulations and make sure we follow them. I was hired to teach."

Was Mrs. Cop-Out correct in her assumption that health regulations should not be her concern?

_____

List three ways in which government regulations about health affect your classroom in a very direct way.

1. _____

2. _____

3. _____

Mrs. Cop-Out was equally upset when her supervisor asked her to identify any children in her classroom with a history of health problems. "It is not my job to snoop through health forms," she insisted. "If there is something wrong with a child, the mother should let me know."

Who is right, Mrs. Cop-Out or her supervisor?

_____

What is the policy in your center regarding teachers' access to health records?

_____

Where are the children's health records kept?

_____

What is the policy in your center regarding sending children home if they are ill?

_____

What are the regulations related to handwashing and disinfecting of toys and surfaces affecting your program?

_____

Frequent and thorough handwashing is the single most important practice in child care programs to promote health and avoid spreading illnesses.

Describe the steps for proper handwashing for child care staff.

_____

_____

_____

_____

List at least four times when teachers need to be sure to wash their own hands.

1. _____

2. _____

3. _____

4. _____

List at least four times when children need to wash their hands while in a child care center.

1. _____

2. _____

3. _____

4. _____

To establish guidelines/policies regarding how to handle health issues, including a record-keeping system

Following health procedures is so much easier when there are clear written policies for the teacher. In some situations, the classroom teacher has to ask the director to write out the health policies of the center.

Mrs. Come-What-May, the director of the Free-and-Easy Child Care Center, was interviewing Ms. Do-It Right, who was applying for a job at Free-and-Easy. The conversation went like this:

Mrs. Come-What-May: "I know you will love working here. Everyone is so relaxed."

Ms. Do-It-Right: "That sounds fine, but before I accept your offer, I would like to ask a few questions."

Mrs. Come-What-May: "Go right ahead."

Ms. Do-It-Right: "What is the responsibility of the teacher in maintaining health records?"

Mrs. Come-What-May: "Oh, don't worry about that. The secretary takes care of all the health records. She gives all the parents a health form to fill out when they come to the center. Most of the parents are pretty good about returning stuff like that, and she always puts them in the file as soon as she gets them back. The teachers never even see them. You know, we are very careful about confidentiality."

Ms. Do-It-Right: "Does the teacher have a way of finding out if a child is allergic to something or has any kind of health problem?"

Mrs. Come-What-May: "Oh, that's no problem. The parents will let you know."

Ms. Do-It-Right: "What is the policy if a child comes to school with a rash or a bad cold?"

Mrs. Come-What-May: "That's the parent's decision. I told you, we have very responsible parents."

Poor Mrs. Come-What-May! She couldn't figure out why Ms. Do-It-Right decided not to accept the job offer. Give three reasons she might have turned the job down.

1. _____

2. _____

3. _____

Objective 4 — To incorporate activities that teach children and families about health, oral/dental hygiene, and nutrition

Carrying Out Practices That Promote Good Health

There was a time when we believed that all illnesses were carried by germs and that if we only knew how to keep germs away from children, we would keep them in good health. Now we know that illness has many causes. Two children may be exposed to the exact same germ. One of the children will catch the disease while the second child will remain healthy. The child who catches the disease has not only been exposed to the disease but has experienced a failure in his body defenses. The disease has challenged the well-being of the child, and his body has not been able to call on its resources to meet the challenge.

Identify six different ways that a classroom teacher can cut down on the spread of germs in the classroom.

1. The teacher can make certain that children:

   _____

   _____

2. The teacher can learn to identify:

   _____

   _____

3. The teacher can be careful about the food that is served in the classroom by making sure that:

   _____

   _____

4. The teacher can teach the children to:

_____

_____

5. The teacher can be sure that she herself:

_____

_____

6. The teacher can make sure that the toys are clean by:

_____

_____

Now identify ways that a teacher can help children build up their
resistance to illness.

1. The teacher can help children and their families learn about a well-balanced diet that includes:

_____

_____

2. The teacher can be sure that the children have regular health and dental check-ups and that:

_____

_____

3. The teacher can serve as a model by:

_____

_____

4. The teacher can help children avoid becoming overtired and stressed by:

_____

_____

5. The teacher can help children maintain good body tone by:

_____

_____

6. The teacher can help children avoid being overheated or chilled by:

_____

_____

Implementing a Health Education Program with Children and Families

In the center, a good teacher has many opportunities in the course of the day to introduce health education.

Here is a transcript of a teacher greeting her group in the morning. As you read it, underline three remarks that the teacher made that could be considered health education.

Teacher: "Good morning, Jeffrey. I am glad that you remembered to wear your sweater. It is cool outside today. Jennifer, you are back in school. We really missed you. Your mommy told me that you had a cold and you had to get lots of rest and drink lots of juice so that you could get better fast. And look at you. You are feeling all better. Bless you, Adam. That was a big sneeze. I like the way you covered your nose and mouth with a tissue."

Adam: "I don't have no cold."

Teacher: "Yes, I know that you don't have a cold. Your mommy told me that you always sneeze when the ragweed is blooming. She told me that you are allergic to ragweed."

Jeffrey: "What's a 'lergic'?"

Teacher: "That's a good question. It is circle time now. Let's talk about it."

It's a good idea to take advantage of spontaneous opportunities to teach health education. It's also a good idea to plan activities with health objectives in mind.

Read the following list of suggested activities. For each activity, select an appropriate health-related objective from the list.

Health-Related Objectives

1. Help children develop a good body image
2. Help children develop self-care skills
3. Help children increase their interest in healthy foods
4. Help children develop positive attitudes toward health care providers

Activities for Preschoolers

1. Collage activities

   a. The teacher or children cut out pictures of healthy and unhealthy foods from magazines.

   b. The children paste the pictures of healthy foods on green construction paper and the pictures of unhealthy foods on red construction paper.

   Objective # _____

2. Body parts game

   a. Play a simple version of Simon Says: "Touch your head, hair, nose, arms, etc."

   Objective # _____

3. Cooking

   a. In small groups, the children cut fruits into small pieces.

   b. For snack, the children serve themselves some fruit in a cup that's half full of plain yogurt.

   Objective # _____

4. Teethbrushing

   a. Provide a child-sized toothbrush with the child's name on it for each child (from parents or donation from dentist).

   b. Implement a daily toothbrushing routine after breakfast or lunch.

   Objective # _____

5. Healthy teeth

   a. Make a tooth puppet.

   b. Let the tooth puppet talk to the children:

   "I like toothpaste."

   "I like to brush my teeth twice a day."

   "I don't like candy. It isn't good for my teeth."

   "I like to chew carrots and apples."

   "I don't like to bite children. It makes me feel sad."

   Objective # _____

6. Food pyramid

   a. Cut out magazine pictures of various foods.

   b. Have the children sort the pictures into basic food groups (cereals and grains, fruits, vegetables, dairy, meats and beans, fats and sweets).

   c. Draw a food pyramid on a large sheet of heavy paper. Let the children paste each food on the correct section of the pyramid.

   d. Hang the food pyramid on the wall.

   Objective # _____

7. Pretend play

   a. Equip the dress-up area with appropriate "doctor" props, such as a stethoscope, white coat, black bag, diploma, toy thermometer, and toy shot syringe.

   b. Encourage the children to play "doctor."

   Objective # _____

To recognize indicators of abuse and/or neglect and follow the reporting policy mandated by the state

Yvonne was a quiet 3-year-old child who seemed to be happiest when she was left alone. She left her mother without protesting in the morning and followed her out the door after school with her head down and no exchange of words. Yvonne avoided messy play, such as pasting, painting, and water play, watching from a distance while the other children got dirty. One day, Yvonne had trouble in the bathroom with a stuck zipper. When the teacher helped Yvonne pull down her jeans, she noticed pronounced black-and-blue marks on Yvonne's upper thighs.

If you were Yvonne's teacher, which of the following steps would you take?

	Yes	No
Ask Yvonne if she was being abused.	☐	☐
Report your concerns to your supervisor.	☐	☐
Discuss your concerns with some of the mothers who live near Yvonne.	☐	☐
Report your observations to the child abuse registry.	☐	☐
Tell Yvonne's mother after school that you were concerned about Yvonne's bruises and her withdrawn behavior and you reported these concerns to an authority in accordance with state law.	☐	☐
Warn Yvonne's mother that she had better watch out or you will report her.	☐	☐

Read over the following list of behaviors that are likely to be associated with neglect and abuse. Place an "N" beside each behavior that is more likely to be associated with neglect and an "A" beside each behavior that is more likely to be associated with abuse.

_____ Clings to adults

_____ Frequently hits other children

_____ Often comes to school without shoes

_____ Is frightened of classroom visitors

_____ Is angry and destructive

_____ Wears the same clothes for several days

To keep oneself healthy and model appropriate wellness behaviors for children and their parents

Children are great copycats. They are much more likely to do what you *do* than what you *say*. Make sure that you model the behaviors you want children to adopt.

Mr. Strongman and Mrs. Not-Me were having a conversation at the child care center as the children were arriving:

Mr. Strongman: "Can you believe Ms. Fit-As-a-Fiddle (the director) won't let us drink soda or coffee in front of the kids anymore?"

Mrs. Not-Me: "I know, but I need this job, so I need to do what she says."

Mr. Strongman: "Yeah, but we need to have something to drink in the middle of the day, too."

Mrs. Not-Me: "I usually slip out of the classroom to get a soda right when the kids are going out on the playground. Then I can have my drink while I walk around on the playground supervising the kids."

List three reasons the director might be upset to hear this conversation.

1. _____

2. _____

3. _____

HEALTHY • *Observation Opportunity*

Name _____

Observe a caregiver in a preschool or infant/toddler setting for 15 minutes. Write a narrative description recording practices by the caregiver that relate to child health.

Example:

Caregiver wiped child's nose.

Threw tissue in a covered container.

Washed her hands.

Praised the child for covering mouth when he coughed.

Helped child wash his hands.

Washed her own hands.

Prepared a snack consisting of a brownie and grapes for each child.

Put a star (*) next to each observation that provides evidence of good health practices.

Observations

_____

_____

_____

_____

_____

_____

_____

_____

_____

_____

_____

_____

HEALTHY • Challenge Activities

Name _____

Challenge 1

Describe, carry out, and evaluate an activity that teaches the children a topic related to health.

Name of Activity: _____

Age Group: _____

Description: What are you going to do?

_____

_____

Objective: What will the children learn from this?

_____

_____

Materials Used:

_____

_____

Procedures: How will you carry out this activity?

_____

_____

_____

Evaluation: Did the activity turn out the way you planned? What changes would you make the next time you do this activity?

_____

_____

_____

Challenge 2

Using the rules and regulations from your local area, find a rule or a regulation that you were unaware existed. Write a short paragraph about this rule or regulation and your plan to be sure that you are enforcing it at your setting.

Description of rule or regulation (include number from the ordinance):

_____

_____

_____

_____

_____

My plan to enforce this rule or regulation in my setting:

_____

_____

_____

_____

_____

_____

_____

_____

_____

_____

_____

_____

_____

HEALTHY • Post-Training Wrap-Up

After completing this unit, review your personal goal and action plan from the beginning of the unit and describe how you accomplished your goal.

_____

_____

_____

_____

List at least three ways in which you changed your behavior as a result of your training in this Functional Area.

1. _____

2. _____

3. _____

HEALTHY • Professional Resource File

Resource Items

Collect the items for the Professional Resource File related to this Functional Area (if applicable). Refer to the pages at the back of this *Trainee's Manual* (pp. 281–283) and to the CDA booklet from the Council for Professional Recognition for specific instructions.

Statement of Competence

Write a short essay of 75 to 150 words, listing one or more goals you have for children and families in the area of health and describing the activities you do to achieve these goals. Describe your experiences in your own words. Be concise. Use "I" statements—for example, "I make sure children always wash their hands after using the bathroom."

For additional information about writing your Statement of Competence, refer to the workbook section at the end of this *Trainee's Manual* (pp. 283–312) and to the CDA booklet from the Council for Professional Recognition.

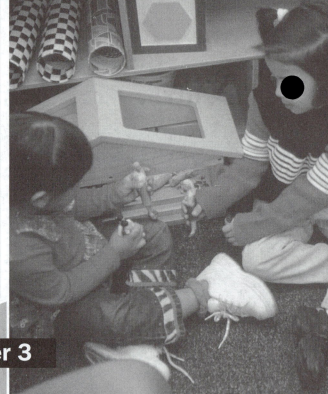

Competency Goal I

To establish and maintain a safe, healthy learning environment

Learning Environment

Overview

A *learning environment* for young children is a place that is conducive to learning and appropriate for the developmental level and learning characteristics of the children.

Rationale

The arrangement of a classroom or family child care setting sets the tone for learning. The selection and setup of play materials, the pictures on the walls, even the way the room is divided—all support beliefs about what and how children should learn. For example, puzzles and sorting toys on low shelves invite children to learn mathematical concepts through play. A pretend play area that can become a "fire station," "circus tent," "grocery store," or "café" invites children to learn about their world by playing together. On the other hand, setting desks in rows and keeping materials on high shelves suggest that learning should be controlled by the teacher and that children should not explore on their own or learn from each other.

Preschoolers need an environment that is safe and welcoming, intriguing but not overwhelming. In a well-planned environment, babies will spend less time crying and more time exploring. Older children will spend less time wandering, fidgeting, and fighting and more time asking questions, working together, and mastering new skills.

Objectives

- **Objective 1** To set up an environment for infants that takes into account the behavioral characteristics, needs, and interests of infants at different stages (0–14 months)

- **Objective 2** To set up an environment that takes into account the behavioral characteristics, needs, and interests of young toddlers (14–24 months)

- **Objective 3** To set up an environment that takes into account the behavioral characteristics, needs, and interests of older toddlers (2 years)

- **Objective 4** To organize and equip a preschool classroom that promotes different kinds of play and learning experiences and that reflects the interests, needs, ability levels, and family backgrounds of the children (3–5 years)

- **Objective 5** To organize and equip a learning environment for a multiage or family child care setting that includes children ages birth through 5

- **Objective 6** To develop a well-balanced daily schedule

- **Objective 7** To set up an outdoor play and learning environment

- **Objective 8** To ensure that the environment works for adults as well as for children

LEARNING ENVIRONMENT • Pretest

Place each preschool item in its proper area.

_____ A. Counting bears

_____ B. Puzzles

_____ C. Magnets

_____ D. Rhythm instruments

_____ E. Wooden blocks

_____ F. Flannelboard stories

_____ G. Play dough

1. Science area
2. Prereading area
3. Music center
4. Block-building center
5. Art area
6. Manipulative play center
7. Math center

Put checkmarks beside the four items that are essential for every infant room.

_____ Cribs

_____ Walkers

_____ Baby swings

_____ Feeding area

_____ Sandbox

_____ Music player

_____ Changing table

Put checkmarks beside the four items that are essential in a room for 1- to 2-year-olds.

_____ Small table and chairs

_____ Push/pull toys

_____ Cardboard, plastic, or vinyl block set

_____ Television set

_____ Barbie dolls

_____ Board books

Put checkmarks beside the four items that are essential in a room for 2- to 3-year-olds.

_____ Whistles

_____ Woodworking area

_____ Pretend play materials

_____ Cars and trucks of different sizes

_____ Board books

_____ Blocks

*Put checkmarks beside the four items that are essential in a room for
3- to 5-year-olds.*

_____ Easels   _____ Puzzles

_____ Television set   _____ Game Boy games

_____ Building blocks   _____ Dress-up clothes

_____ Workbooks

Answer True (T) or False (F) to each of the following questions.

_____ 1. In a toddler classroom, it is a good idea to have soft materials, such as stuffed animals, quilts, and mats.

_____ 2. Noisy and quiet areas should be right next to each other.

_____ 3. *Developmentally appropriate practice* is the term used to describe ways of teaching and organizing children's experiences that take into account the age and capabilities of each child.

_____ 4. The Reggio Emilia approach encourages children to use their own symbol notation, drawing and painting, dancing and pantomime, and various kinds of three-dimensional modeling to express themselves.

_____ 5. A High/Scope classroom is set up with learning centers that invite children to explore materials and engage in developmentally appropriate activities.

LEARNING ENVIRONMENT • Self-Assessment

Indicate how you feel about your skills and abilities in each of the following categories by checking the appropriate column.

	Pretraining		
	Strong	**Satisfactory**	***Needs Improvement***
I can set up an environment that takes into account the behavioral characteristics, needs, and interests of infants at different stages.	☐	☐	☐
I can set up an environment that takes into account the behavioral characteristics, needs, and interests of young toddlers.	☐	☐	☐
I can set up an environment that takes into account the behavioral characteristics, needs, and interests of older toddlers.	☐	☐	☐
I can organize and equip a preschool classroom that promotes different kinds of play and learning experiences and that reflects the interests, needs, ability levels, and family backgrounds of the children.	☐	☐	☐
I can organize and equip a learning environment for a multiage or family child care setting that includes children ages birth through 5.	☐	☐	☐
I can set up an outdoor play and learning environment.	☐	☐	☐
I can ensure that the environment works for adults as well as for children.	☐	☐	☐

Competency Goal I • To establish and maintain a safe, healthy learning environment

LEARNING ENVIRONMENT • Pretraining Personal Goal

Based on your pretraining self-assessment, write a personal goal for this Functional Area and an action plan describing how you will accomplish the goal.

Goal _____

_____

_____

_____

Action Plan _____

_____

_____

_____

_____

_____

_____

_____

_____

_____

_____

_____

_____

Save your goal and action plan for the end of this unit so you will be able to answer these questions: How did you accomplish your goal? And how has your behavior changed based on your training?

To set up an environment for infants that takes into account the behavioral characteristics, needs, and interests of infants at different stages (0–14 months)

Setting up an infant room takes a lot of thought. Young infants who are not mobile have different needs than older infants in terms of play space and floor surfaces. Rooms for young infants need cribs, changing tables that are close to a water source and convenient for their caregivers, and washable floormats for out-of the-crib playtimes. They also need a nearby refrigerator for bottle storage and cubbies for changes of clothes. As infants learn to crawl, creep, stand, and cruise, their list of basic needs grows longer. They need safe places to crawl and creep, unbreakable mirrors, furniture to pull up on, washable flooring, feeding tables, and low, sturdy shelves with toys that they can reach.

The director of the Bundle and Cuddle Preschool was planning to add a baby room. Once she had purchased all the basic furnishings, she decided to draw the layout for her classroom. She was quite pleased with her drawing and could not understand why the parents of the babies didn't share her enthusiasm. See the following sketch of the classroom that the director planned to create.

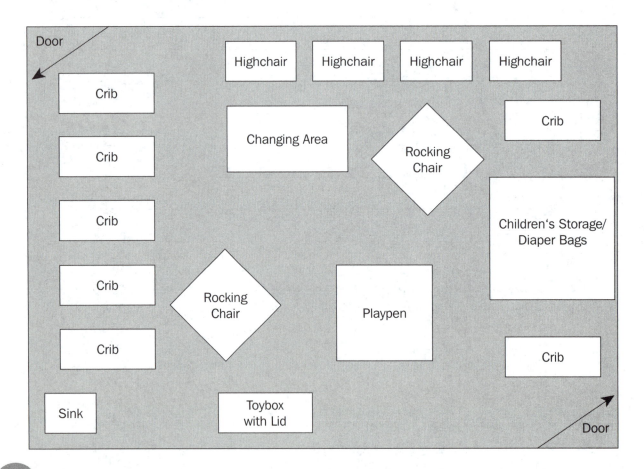

Describe at least three changes in the classroom that would likely please the parents. Give a reason for each of your suggestions.

1. _____

2. _____

3. _____

Arranging an infant room is always a difficult challenge. When there are eight or more infants of different ages sharing the same space, it is especially difficult to arrange the room so that it accommodates the needs of all of the children, whether or not they are mobile. Infant caregivers are faced with the problem of arranging the infant room so that it can be used for both waking and sleeping activities.

One solution, suggested by Mrs. Hurdle-Jumper, is to place the cribs in the center of the room and create play spaces for mobile infants on one side of the room. A second solution, suggested by Mrs. Make-Do, is to place the eight cribs in a semicircle on one side of the room, leaving the central area of the room for diapering and feeding and the far end for play. The play area for mobile infants is a double-sized playpen that gives them a space to creep and pull up. The play area for nonmobile infants is a clean sheet or a washable mat.

Describe an advantage and a problem that may be associated with each teacher's solution.

1. _____

2. _____

Might another solution work out better? If so, describe it.

_____

_____

_____

_____

_____

_____

_____

To set up an environment that takes into account the behavioral characteristics, needs, and interests of young toddlers (14–24 months)

Setting up a room for young toddlers between the ages of 1 and 2 presents a whole new set of problems. Young toddlers are becoming increasingly more active and more social. They want to play with their peers, to show off their new physical prowess, and to join their peers in imitative play. Once young toddlers learn to walk, they will try new variations, carrying large, heavy things, pushing furniture around, and climbing on anything they can manage to get up on.

Mrs. Go-the-Whole-Mile decided to arrange her classroom so that the children would have plenty of opportunity to practice their new motor skills. Here is a list of the items that she decided to put in the classroom.

Put an "X" before each item you feel she should leave at home.

_____ A set of large cardboard blocks

_____ A trampoline

_____ An old carpet sweeper she wasn't using anymore

_____ A stepladder

_____ A rocking boat

_____ A big toybox

_____ A dishwashing tub

_____ A pop-up push toy

To set up an environment that takes into account the behavioral characteristics, needs, and interests of older toddlers (2 years)

Two-year-olds enjoy playing with one or two friends, running, chasing, sliding, swinging, playing Follow the Leader, climbing, practicing their jumping skills, and riding on play cars, trucks, or Big Wheels. While 2-year-olds enjoy playing with their friends, they are not very good at sharing and will often get into hassles when friends refuse to share favorite toys.

Mrs. Clueless is complaining to the director about the problem that she is having with the 2-year-olds on the playground. She decided that she needed to order more toys for the playground and brought her director a long "wish list" that included these items:

> 5 new wheel toys
>
> 5 new trucks
>
> 6 large play cars
>
> 3 more slides
>
> 6 rocking horses

The director was not at all impressed with the list. "Maybe," she said, "instead of buying duplicates of everything that you already have, you could find some toys that would encourage children to play together cooperatively."

Poor Mrs. Clueless was stumped. Please help her by listing three outdoor toys that would encourage toddlers to play together.

1. _____

2. _____

3. _____

To organize and equip a preschool classroom that promotes different kinds of play and learning experiences and that reflects the interests, needs, ability levels, and family backgrounds of the children (3–5 years)

Arranging a classroom into interest centers supports the philosophy that children learn through exploration and discovery with the help of the teacher as a facilitator. The teacher provides opportunities for children to enjoy self-selected activities and to learn through active involvement. The classroom is divided into different areas, with each area reflecting the type of activity that takes place.

Interest centers are semienclosed spaces where several children can work side by side. Materials are placed on shelves or on low tables, allowing children to choose activities without requiring help from the teacher. As a facilitator, the teacher moves from center to center, answering questions, giving suggestions to individual children, and joining children in play.

Here are some interest centers that can be set up in child care settings. What should each include?

A construction play or block-building center that includes:

_____

A science and discovery center that includes:

_____

An art center that includes:

_____

A play and learn or manipulative play center that includes:

_____

A reading corner that includes:

_____

A dress-up center (sometimes called "Grandma's attic") that includes:

_____

A housekeeping center that includes:

_____

Now let's visit your own classroom. If you already have interest centers, list them. If you do not have interest centers, list the centers in your "dream" classroom.

1. _____

2. _____

3. _____

4. _____

5. _____

6. _____

To organize and equip a learning environment for a multiage or family child care setting that includes children ages birth through 5

In the United States, as well as in other countries, the concept of multiage grouping—where children from infancy through 5 years old interact in the same setting—is gaining popularity. Although multiage grouping may take place either in a center or in a home, setting up family child care in a home setting is especially appealing to parents. Licensed family child care homes, where the caregiver is trained in early childhood, are viable child care alternatives.

Mrs. Home Sweet Home was the operator of a small family child care home. In the past, she had only taken infants and young toddlers. But as the children became older, the parents and the children became very comfortable with the situation at the family child care home. The parents wanted their children to stay with Mrs. Home Sweet Home. Mrs. Home Sweet Home had also grown very attached to the children. She had had some of the children since they were 8 weeks old.

Now Mrs. Home Sweet Home had children from 4 months through 3 years old in her care that all had different needs and abilities. It seemed as though when the infants needed to be fed or changed, the preschool-age children wanted to play outdoors. When Mrs. Home Sweet Home would answer the phone, the toddlers would try to take away the toys from the 3-year-olds, who would then hit the toddlers over the head to get their toy back. The 3-year-old children no longer needed a morning nap, but the infants still did.

Mrs. Home Sweet Home had always made hot lunches for the children through a local food program, but this time of day had become so hectic that she did not know what to do. Mrs. Home Sweet Home knew that the preschool children needed to experience some additional creative experiences, but she was afraid that the infants might eat the play dough or paint. Storytime was always a disaster, with all of the children wanting to sit in her lap.

Another problem was keeping the small toys out of the reach of the infants and toddlers. Just when she thought she had it figured out, the toddlers started to climb on the shelves to get at the small pieces.

Mrs. Home Sweet Home came to realize that she needed to figure out some strategies for meeting everybody's needs, but she didn't know where to start.

Help Mrs. Home Sweet Home come up with four organizational strategies to help her get through the day.

1. _____

_____

2. _____

_____

3. _____

_____

4. _____

_____

Objective 6
To develop a well-balanced daily schedule

Mrs. Coddler was the head teacher in the infant room. Mrs. Hold-Tight was placing her child in child care for the first time. Before she left the center, Mrs. Hold-Tight asked Mrs. Coddler what her schedule was for the older infants. "No different from my schedule for the younger infants," Mrs. Coddler assured her. "Babies don't need a schedule. I feed them when they are hungry. I change them when they are dirty. And when they want to play, I bring them a toy or two."

Do you agree or disagree that there is no need for a schedule when the babies are under 1 year of age? Support your opinion in a short paragraph.

_____

_____

_____

_____

_____

_____

_____

Toddlers

Mrs. Wipe-Up was working on a schedule for her toddlers. This is the schedule she developed:

8:00–9:00	Block play
9:00–11:30	Outdoor play
11:30–12:00	Bathroom and handwashing
12:30–1:00	Lunch
1 :00–3:00	Naptime
3:00–3:30	Toileting time
3:30–5:00	Free play outdoors

Identify three problems with this schedule.

1. _____

2. _____

3. _____

Preschool

The following conversation took place at the First Try Child Care Center:

Mrs. Hyper: "I don't know what got into the children today. They were bouncing off the walls. We did our usual morning exercises, followed by a lively music session, where the children danced around the room. Then we went out on the playground, where they played some sort of fun 'monster' chase game. And then we came inside for band. (We finally got the drums I ordered.) By lunchtime, the children were bouncing off the walls."

Mrs. Droop: "I had trouble with my class today, too. We started Show and Tell, and each child had a chance to talk about their weekend. Then we drew pictures in their day books, and then I read a chapter from *Alice in Wonderland*, and then they went to work at their desks, where we worked on writing the letter 'D.' I let the children choose whatever crayon they wanted to color the D's, but I just couldn't get them to calm down."

Help these two teachers manage their classes by discussing changes in their schedules.

Changes for Mrs. Hyper

1. _____

2. _____

3. _____

Changes for Mrs. Droop

1. _____

2. _____

3. _____

Objective 7 — To set up an outdoor play and learning environment

While the amount of time spent in outdoor play depends on both the weather and the ages of the children, all children benefit from spending time out of doors.

Look over the following list of playground features and equipment. Before each item, write the age or ages for which the feature or equipment is appropriate. If something is not appropriate for any child under 5, leave it blank. Use the initials "I" for infants, "T" for toddlers, and "P" for preschool children. You will find that for some of the items, you may want to use more than one initial.

_____ Trampoline   _____ Playhouses

_____ Adequate shade   _____ Strollers

_____ Tricycles   _____ Wagons

_____ Sandboxes with covers   _____ A 5-foot fence

_____ Low balance beam (4" wide) _____ 45 square feet of space
                                       for every child

To ensure that the environment works for adults as well as for children

Although child caregivers are likely to place the needs of the children over their own needs, all caregivers can do a better job if there are spaces within the center set aside that are appropriate for adults.

Look over the following lists. One list is for parents, and the other list is for caregivers. Make a check in front of each item that you feel is very important and a circle in front of each item that would be nice to have if there was enough money and enough space. Leave blank any item that you feel is not really necessary.

Caregivers List

_____ A bathroom that is separate from the bathrooms for the children

_____ A secure place where caregivers can put their purses and other personal items

_____ A room with comfortable seating where caregivers can hold planning sessions

_____ A desk for each teacher

_____ A bulletin board where parents and teachers can exchange messages

_____ A telephone in every classroom

_____ A separate lunchroom

Parents List

_____ A list of the telephone numbers of every child in the classroom

_____ A bulletin board where parents can exchange notes

_____ A chair where parents can sit when visiting their children

_____ A place in the classroom where parents can display pictures from their homes or items associated with their own cultures

_____ A place in the center where parents can get fresh coffee

_____ A parking place right in front of the center

_____ A handicapped-accessible bathroom

LEARNING ENVIRONMENT • *Observation Opportunity*

Name _____

Observe a classroom other than the one in which you work.

Age Group _____

Describe the room arrangement with attention to:	Observations
Interest centers (List)	_____ _____ _____
Arrangement of furniture (Look for traffic patterns in the classroom, strategies used to section off centers, locations of centers in the room)	_____ _____ _____
Materials in the room (Consider appropriateness, variety, state of repair, and accessibility to children)	_____ _____ _____
Visibility of all areas to the teacher	_____ _____
The wall displays (Consider eye-level location and individuality in children's work)	_____ _____ _____
The presence of soft materials	_____ _____ _____
The general attractiveness of the room	_____ _____

LEARNING ENVIRONMENT • Challenge Activities

Name _____

Challenge 1

Select three of the interest centers/areas in your classroom. Describe eight new props or materials that you would like to add to these centers. Using teacher supply catalogues, include the price for each item. Give your rationale for why each item is important to include.

Setting: (circle one)

Infants   Toddlers   Preschoolers   School Age   Family Child Care

Interest Center 1 _____

1. _____ Price _____

   Rationale _____

2. _____ Price _____

   Rationale _____

3. _____ Price _____

   Rationale _____

4. _____ Price _____

   Rationale _____

5. _____ Price _____

   Rationale _____

6. _____ Price _____

   Rationale _____

7. _____ Price _____

   Rationale _____

8. _____ Price _____

   Rationale _____

Interest Center 2 _____

1. _____ Price _____

   Rationale _____

2. _____ Price _____

   Rationale _____

3. _____ Price _____

   Rationale _____

4. _____ Price _____

   Rationale _____

5. _____ Price _____

   Rationale _____

6. _____ Price _____

   Rationale _____

7. _____ Price _____

   Rationale _____

8. _____ Price _____

   Rationale _____

Interest Center 3 _____

1. _____ Price _____

   Rationale _____

2. _____ Price _____

   Rationale _____

3. _____ Price _____

   Rationale _____

Competency Goal I • To establish and maintain a safe, healthy learning environment

4. _____ Price _____

Rationale _____

5. _____ Price _____

Rationale _____

6. _____ Price _____

Rationale _____

7. _____ Price _____

Rationale _____

8. _____ Price _____

Rationale _____

Challenge 2

Write out the schedule that would meet the needs of the children in your age group.

Ages of Children _____

Time	Activity
_____	_____
_____	_____
_____	_____
_____	_____
_____	_____
_____	_____
_____	_____
_____	_____
_____	_____

Challenge 3

Draw your ideal room setup. Refer to Chapter 3 in the textbook for considerations for your age group.

Ages of Children _____

LEARNING ENVIRONMENT • Post-Training Wrap-Up

After completing this unit, review your personal goal and action plan from the beginning of the unit and describe how you accomplished your goal.

_____

_____

_____

_____

List at least three ways in which you changed your behavior as a result of your training in this Functional Area.

1. _____

2. _____

3. _____

LEARNING ENVIRONMENT • Professional Resource File

Resource Items

Collect the items for the Professional Resource File related to this Functional Area (if applicable). Refer to the pages at the back of this *Trainee's Manual* (pp. 281–283) and to the CDA booklet from the Council for Professional Recognition for specific instructions.

Statement of Competence

Write a short essay of 75 to 150 words, listing one or more goals you have for children and families in the area of learning environment and describing the activities you do to achieve these goals. Describe your experiences in your own words. Be concise. Use "I" statements—for example, "I arrange my classroom into activity areas where small groups of children can play and learn."

For additional information about writing your Statement of Competence, refer to the workbook section at the end of this *Trainee's Manual* (pp. 283–312) and to the CDA booklet from the Council for Professional Recognition.

The statements you have written for the chapters Safe, Healthy, and Learning Environment together make up the Competency Goal Statement for Goal I: To establish and maintain a safe, healthy learning environment.

Chapter 4

Physical

Overview

Physical development refers to the development of gross-motor or large-muscle skills, such as crawling, walking, and batting, and of fine-motor or small-muscle skills, involved in tasks such as eating, writing, cutting, and drawing.

Rationale

Because young children are always on the go, parents and teachers are apt to relax about their physical development. You might hear them say, "Just let them run around and play, and they'll get all the exercise they need."

It is true that each child has his own developmental timetable and that he will sit up and walk and run according to this timetable, no matter how we arrange his environment. But physical development involves a lot more than learning how to walk and run. Physical development is an important facet of the whole developmental process. The child's mind and body work together.

The development of motor skills contributes to the development of social and emotional skills, language, and problem-solving skills. The teacher plays an important role in supporting physical development by preparing the environment and by providing a variety of appropriate equipment, activities, and opportunities.

Objectives

● **Objective 1** To recognize expectable sequences in small- and large-muscle development in infancy and describe materials and activities that will enhance this development

● **Objective 2** To recognize expectable sequences in small- and large-muscle development in young toddlers and describe materials and activities that will enhance this development

● **Objective 3** To recognize expectable sequences in small- and large-muscle development in older toddlers and describe materials and activities that will enhance this development

● **Objective 4** To recognize expectable sequences in small- and large-muscle development in preschoolers and describe materials and activities that will enhance this development

● **Objective 5** To identify materials and activities that will enhance the physical development of children with special needs

PHYSICAL • Pretest

Match each skill with the description of the activity that will promote it.

_____ 1. Places pegs in a pegboard

_____ 2. Throws a large ball into a basket

_____ 3. Screws a bottle top onto a bottle

_____ 4. Picks up a Cheerio to eat using the thumb and first finger

_____ 5. Walks on a line

_____ 6. Completes a forward somersault

_____ 7. Wads up a piece of paper using only one hand

_____ 8. Jumps over a rope

_____ 9. Pushes a swing very gently and then very hard and predicts how high the swing will go on one push

_____ 10. An infant is pulled up to a sitting position with no head lag

_____ 11. Stands on one foot briefly

A. Finger/thumb opposition (pincer grasp)

B. Discovers relationships and makes predictions

C. Head control

D. Strength of grasp

E. Motor coordination

F. Jumping skill

G. Eye/hand coordination

H. Wrist coordination or swivel

I. Dynamic balance

J. Static balance

K. Throwing skill

List one large-muscle and one small-muscle skill that you would expect a child in each age group to have achieved.

Age Group	Small-Muscle Skill	Large-Muscle Skill
0–6 months	_____	_____
12–24 months	_____	_____
2–3 years	_____	_____
3–5 years	_____	_____

PHYSICAL • Self-Assessment

Indicate how you feel about your skills and abilities in each of the following categories by checking the appropriate column.

	Pretraining		
	Strong	**Satisfactory**	**Needs Improvement**
I recognize expectable sequences in small- and large-muscle development in infancy and can describe materials and activities that will enhance this development.	☐	☐	☐
I recognize expectable sequences in small- and large-muscle development in young toddlers and can describe materials and activities that will enhance this development.	☐	☐	☐
I recognize expectable sequences in small- and large-muscle development in older toddlers and can describe materials and activities that will enhance this development.	☐	☐	☐
I recognize expectable sequences in small- and large-muscle development in preschoolers and can describe materials and activities that will enhance this development.	☐	☐	☐
I can identify appropriate materials activities that will enhance the physical development of children with special needs.	☐	☐	☐

PHYSICAL • Pretraining Personal Goal

Based on your pretraining self-assessment, write a personal goal for this Functional Area and an action plan describing how you will accomplish the goal.

Goal _____

_____

_____

_____

Action Plan _____

_____

_____

_____

_____

_____

_____

_____

_____

_____

_____

_____

Save your goal and action plan for the end of this unit so you will be able to answer these questions: How did you accomplish your goal? And how has your behavior changed based on your training?

To recognize expectable sequences in small- and large-muscle development in infancy and describe materials and activities that will enhance this development

Although specialists are learning more and more about the amazing capabilities of infants, compared with other animal species, humans are born helpless and immature and are completely dependent on their caregivers. During the first year, however, infants make amazing progress, learning new motor skills almost before our eyes.

Small-muscle and large-muscle skills develop at a rapid rate between birth and 1 year old. From birth, babies have the ability to grasp a finger when it is put into their fist. In the beginning, grasping is a reflex, but during the first year, grasping, as well as many other critical small-muscle skills, develop in a predictable sequence.

Mrs. Get-with-It-Kid was a new aide in the Babes-Are-Our-Thing Nursery. She had no experience with infants but had some very strong ideas about what infants should be able to do. She was especially intent on infants learning to feed themselves. She put each of the babies into a feeding chair, including a 5-month-old, a 6-month-old, an 8-month-old, and a 10-month-old. She was shocked by the fact that not one of these babies had any idea about how to eat with a spoon. Worse than that, she found most of the babies couldn't even feed themselves a small cracker when she put it on the table.

When the director of the nursery came into the room, she was even more shocked. Her first instinct was to fire Mrs. Get-with-It-Kid, but then she decided that maybe with more training, she would be able to handle the job. She gave Mrs. Get-with-It-Kid a quiz on small-muscle development in infants and told her to find out the answers.

Poor Mrs. Get-with-It-Kid was at a complete loss. In the following list, please help her match each skill described on the left side with the appropriate age listed on the right side.

Skill

Expected Age of Accomplishment

_____ 1. Uses a pincer grasp to pick up small objects

_____ 2. Is able to bring her hand to her mouth

_____ 3. Can reach and swat a ring on her cradle gym

_____ 4. Uses a raking motion to pick up a small toy

_____ 5. Points to an object using one finger

_____ 6. Is able to put a pacifier in his mouth

_____ 7. Picks up a small block and drops it into a cup

A. Birth–1 month

B. 1–2 months

C. 2–4 months

D. 4–6 months

E. 6–8 months

F. 8–10 months

G. 10–12 months

Objective 2 · To recognize expectable sequences in small- and large-muscle development in young toddlers and describe materials and activities that will enhance this development

Between 1 and 2 years old, children work hard practicing all of the motor skills they acquire.

List three motor skills that children achieve between 1 and 2 years of age.

1. _____

2. _____

3. _____

Mrs. Plan-Ahead, the teacher of young toddlers between 1 and 2 years old, had just completed a course in child development. She learned that young toddlers were developing small-muscle skills at a very fast rate. They were learning how to pound using an instrument, how to probe with one finger, how to swivel their wrist, how to stack, how to use both hands to pull things apart, how to pour, and how to crank. Her problem was that she couldn't for the life of her figure out what materials she could use to help the children practice these new skills.

Please give her some good ideas.

Probing with one finger _____

Swiveling their wrists _____

Stacking one object on top of another _____

Using an instrument to make a mark _____

Pouring _____

Cranking _____

To recognize expectable sequences in small- and large-muscle development in older toddlers and describe materials and activities that will enhance this development

By 2 years, most children have just about mastered the art of walking and are ready to experiment. They stand on their tiptoes, walk sideways and backward, step over barriers (a rock, a toy, a baby sister), roll down hills, and turn around in circles. Two-year-olds love to climb and jump but haven't learned to tell the difference between safe jumping places and dangerous ones. As a matter of fact, safety is a big concern now. The 2-year-old is strong enough and agile enough to get into risky places yet not experienced enough to know when to stop climbing or where not to jump.

List three new large-muscle skills that children develop between 2 and 3 years of age.

1. _____

2. _____

3. _____

Mr. Know-How was working with a group of 2-year-olds. He was really skilled at finding activities that children enjoyed but was at a complete loss when anyone asked him what the children were learning when they engaged in different activities. One day, a parent came to visit and was really annoyed when she saw the children playing happily in different parts of the room, rather than learning how to recite the alphabet, recognize letters, and count objects.

Mr. Know-How knew that the children were engaged in a lot of different age-appropriate activities and were having a good time, but he didn't know how to explain to this overanxious mother the benefits of these activities.

Help Mr. Know-How describe the small-muscle and large-muscle skills that the children were learning as they engaged in the following activities.

In the art center, one child was painting on an easel.

_____

_____

In the reading center, Tommy was turning the pages of a picture book.

_____

_____

In the block area, three children were building towers with cardboard blocks.

_____

_____

In the pretend play area, two children were playing "birthday party." They pretended to pour lemonade into their cups and used a plastic fork to pretend to eat birthday cake.

_____

_____

In the manipulative play area, one child was putting together a puzzle. A second child was using a hammer to pound down the pegs in a workbench.

_____

_____

In the music area, a child was winding up the music box.

_____

_____

In the dress-up area, a child was playing "firefighter" and snapping up her raincoat.

_____

_____

To recognize expectable sequences in small- and large-muscle development in preschoolers and describe materials and activities that will enhance this development

Three-Year-Olds

The 3-year-old is apt to be a bit more careful about herself. She might even be a little afraid of trying out new things. Once she is comfortable in a group, however, she will become a great copycat. She loves to play Follow-the-Leader games, like arms up and down, touch your head, and touch your toes. A favorite game is turning around in circles until she's dizzy. The 3-year-old has improved her jumping ability. Now she can jump over a plank, jump off the second stair, and walk sideways across a plank or balance beam. She may try to hop but is usually not too successful, although she does manage to stand on one foot for a few seconds. She can throw a large ball using two hands, but it doesn't go very far or very straight. It seems, sometimes, that she enjoys throwing for the sake of throwing and isn't very concerned about where the ball happens to land.

Complete the following sentences.

1. Most 3-year-olds can catch a large ball if:

   _____

   _____

   _____

2. When 3-year-olds are on a swing, they usually:

_____

_____

_____

3. When 3-year-olds walk up stairs, they usually:

_____

_____

_____

Four-Year-Olds

A typical 4-year-old is full of energy and curiosity. He has to move around, push, pull, tug, hit, and throw. This continuous motion is not only his way of using up energy; more important, it is his way of learning new things about himself and his world. When the teacher says "Sit still," she is asking for the impossible. "Sit still and don't move" means the same thing to a 4-year-old as "Sit still and don't learn."

Movement for the 4-year-old accomplishes three very important things. First, it gives her information about the things around her and their relationship to each other. She learns the meanings of *high* and *low* by reaching for the toys on the top shelf. Second, it gives her new information about her body and the things she can do with it. She learns that she can balance on one foot, walk forward and backward across a plank or balance beam, take a big jump forward and a small jump backward, throw a beanbag at a target, and catch a big ball by clasping it in her hands. Third, and most important, it provides opportunities for fun. In the process of playing games like Follow the Leader and Monkey See, Monkey Do, the child discovers how to get along with children, how to put her energy to work, and how to satisfy her endless curiosity.

Give four reasons for including movement activities as part of your classroom routine for 4-year-olds.

1. _____

2. _____

3. _____

4. _____

Five-Year-Olds

As we trace the development of large-muscle skills from infancy to 5 years old, we recognize that there are many different skills that the child must achieve. Let us think about how these skills can be categorized.

Mrs. See-for-Yourself decided to spend the day in her daughter's preschool classroom. She had read the school brochure very carefully and wanted to make sure that her daughter was getting everything that the brochure promised. At the end of the day, she confronted the classroom teacher.

"I was really impressed by a lot of the things that go on in this classroom—the art activities, the circle time, the dramatic play—but I didn't see anything going on that could help children develop physical skills. It says in the brochure that daily activities are planned to enhance motor skill development."

"You are right," the classroom teacher agreed. "You did not see the children practicing large-muscle skills. You see, we practice large-muscle skills outside, but this week, it has rained every day."

Unquestionably, Mrs. See-for-Yourself had a good point. Although the playground provides more opportunities for the development of motor skills than the classroom, children need opportunities to practice large-muscle skills whether or not the sun is shining.

Help this classroom teacher identify indoor activities that can be carried out to develop large-muscle skills. List two activities for each skill area.

Indoor activities to help children develop dynamic balance

   1. _____

     _____

   2. _____

     _____

Indoor activities to help children with rhythm and coordination

   1. _____

     _____

   2. _____

     _____

Indoor activities to help children develop jumping skills

1. _____

_____

2. _____

_____

objective 5

To identify appropriate materials and activities that will enhance the physical development of children with special needs

Jeremy was a 3½-year-old boy new to the child care center. When his mother enrolled him, she mentioned that he had been assessed by the local Child Find and was found to have some minor motor delays. You had noted this as well when you observed him during his first week in your class. He also seemed to be getting frustrated with some of the activities you had planned. For example, he usually avoided cutting with scissors and gave up easily when playing on the playground equipment.

Using the Developmental Picture from the textbook, adapt two small-muscle activities and two large-muscle activities so that Jeremy can be successful in your classroom.

1. Small-muscle skill

_____

Activity for Jeremy

_____

_____

2. Small-muscle skill

_____

Activity for Jeremy

_____

_____

1. Large-muscle skill

   _____

   Activity for Jeremy

   _____

   _____

2. Large-muscle skill

   _____

   Activity for Jeremy

   _____

   _____

PHYSICAL • Observation Opportunity

Name _____

Observe an infant, toddler, or preschool child for 10 minutes. Based on your observation, complete the following statements.

The child demonstrated the ability to achieve the following task that required hand/eye coordination:

_____

_____

_____

The child demonstrated the ability to perform the following large-muscle activities:

_____

_____

_____

The child demonstrated the ability to perform the following activities that required small-muscle coordination:

_____

_____

_____

The child demonstrated the following activities requiring static (standing still) or dynamic (in-motion) balance:

_____

_____

_____

The child attempted but did not succeed with the following physical challenge:

_____

_____

_____

PHYSICAL • Challenge Activities

Name _____

Challenge 1

Compare the physical development of the oldest child and the youngest child in your group, noting the differences in small- and large-muscle skills (fine- and gross-motor development). Provide at least six examples.

Skill Observed	Child 1: Age in months ____	Child 2: Age in months ____

Challenge 2

Describe, carry out, and evaluate a large-muscle activity that can be done indoors on a rainy day.

Name of Activity: _____

Age Group: _____

Description: What are you going to do?

_____

_____

_____

_____

Objective: What will the children learn from this?

_____

_____

_____

Materials Used:

_____

_____

Procedures: How will you carry out this activity?

_____

_____

_____

Evaluation: Did the activity turn out the way you planned? What changes would you make the next time you do this activity?

_____

_____

_____

PHYSICAL • Post-Training Wrap-Up

After completing this unit, review your personal goal and action plan from the beginning of the unit and describe how you accomplished your goal.

_____

_____

_____

_____

List at least three ways in which you have changed your behavior as a result of your training in this Functional Area.

1. _____

2. _____

3. _____

PHYSICAL • Professional Resource File

Resource Items

Collect the items for the Professional Resource File related to this Functional Area (if applicable). Refer to the pages at the back of this *Trainee's Manual* (pp. 281–283) and to the CDA booklet from the Council for Professional Recognition for specific instructions.

Statement of Competence

Write a short essay of 75 to 150 words, listing one or more goals you have for promoting children's physical development and describing the activities you do to achieve these goals. Describe your experiences in your own words. Be concise. Use "I" statements—for example, "I make sure children have many opportunities to enjoy active play outdoors. I provide a wide variety of manipulative materials to help children develop small-muscle control."

For additional information about writing your Statement of Competence, refer to the workbook section at the end of this *Trainee's Manual* (pp. 283–312) and to the CDA booklet from the Council for Professional Recognition.

Competency Goal II
To advance physical and intellectual competence

Chapter 5

Cognitive

Overview

Cognitive, or *intellectual, development* refers to the child's growing ability to give meaning to experience, to reason, to acquire knowledge, and to problem solve.

Rationale

As the child interacts with the environment, she discovers how things work. As she interacts with people, she acquires patterns, language, information, and ideas. As she tries to make sense of her experiences, she develops new concepts and modifies old ways of thinking.

Although what each child learns is unique, the underlying concepts are developed in a predictable sequence. Each new step provides the foundation for the next.

Objectives

- **Objective 1**   To recognize expectable sequences in cognitive development in infancy and describe materials and activities that will enhance this development

- **Objective 2**   To recognize expectable sequences in cognitive development in young toddlers and describe materials and activities that will enhance this development

- **Objective 3**   To recognize expectable sequences in cognitive development in older toddlers and describe materials and activities that will enhance this development

- **Objective 4**   To recognize expectable sequences in cognitive development in preschool children and describe materials and activities that will enhance this development

- **Objective 5**   To learn how to create a preschool environment that encourages exploration, curiosity, and critical thinking

- **Objective 6**   To learn techniques for introducing meaningful themes into preschool classrooms

COGNITIVE • Pretest

Match each activity on the left with the skill it fosters.

_____ 1. The children are given items of different sizes and asked to try to fit each item (one at a time) into a pint container. The children are asked to tell why some items fit and others do not.

_____ 2. The children are given a set of shapes and asked to sort them.

_____ 3. The children's dramatic play area is transformed into a "grocery store" with empty food containers, shopping carts, bags, a cash register, play money, pads for writing lists, and so on.

A. Classification

B. Problem solving

C. Concept development

Pick an item from the right-hand column to identify each description in the left-hand column.

_____ 1. Timothy counted "1, 2, 3, 6, 2, 1, 10."

_____ 2. Tina was asked to pass out cookies. Miss Anton told her to be sure to give one cookie to each child. There were 10 children and 12 cookies. Tina kept passing the cookies around until she had none left.

_____ 3. Miss Alice asked Fred to count to 5. He counted "1, 2, 3, 4, 5." Then she asked him to take off his shoe and count his toes. "1, 2, 3, 4, 5, 6, 7, 8" he counted proudly, touching his toes as he recited the numbers.

_____ 4. "How many crayons do you have, Judith?" asked Mr. Gillespie (knowing full well she had six). "1, 2, 3, 4, 5, 6" Judith counted aloud, carefully touching a crayon as she recited each number. "I have lots of crayons—3, 5, and 6 crayons," Judith answered, matter of factly.

A. Lacks one-to-one correspondence.

B. Does not recognize that the answer to "How many?" is the number reached in the count.

C. Unable to count by rote.

D. Counts by rote but can't count objects (i.e., does not recognize that each object gets one and only one count).

Provide answers to each of the following.

1. List three materials found in a preschool classroom that promote appropriate premath skills.

   (1) _____

   (2) _____

   (3) _____

2. List three materials found in a preschool classroom that promote science exploration.

   (1) _____

   (2) _____

   (3) _____

3. List three sensory materials suitable for toddlers learning to explore their environment.

   (1) _____

   (2) _____

   (3) _____

COGNITIVE • Self-Assessment

Indicate how you feel about your skills and abilities in each of the following categories by checking the appropriate column.

	Pretraining		
	Strong	**Satisfactory**	**Needs Improvement**
I recognize expectable sequences in cognitive development in infancy and can describe materials and activities that will enhance this development.	☐	☐	☐
I recognize expectable sequences in cognitive development in young toddlers and can describe materials and activities that will enhance this development.	☐	☐	☐
I recognize expectable sequences in cognitive development in older toddlers and can describe materials and activities that will enhance this development.	☐	☐	☐
I recognize expectable sequences in cognitive development in preschool children and can describe materials and activities that will enhance this development.	☐	☐	☐
I know how to create a preschool environment that encourages exploration, curiosity, and critical thinking.	☐	☐	☐
I know how to introduce meaningful themes into preschool classrooms.	☐	☐	☐

COGNITIVE • Pretraining Personal Goal

Based on your pretraining self-assessment, write a personal goal for this Functional Area and an action plan describing how you will accomplish the goal.

Goal _____

_____

_____

_____

Action Plan _____

_____

_____

_____

_____

_____

_____

_____

_____

_____

_____

Save your goal and action plan for the end of this unit so you will be able to answer these questions: How did you accomplish your goal? And how has your behavior changed based on your training?

To recognize expectable sequences in cognitive development in infancy and describe materials and activities that will enhance this development

From the moment of birth, infants struggle to organize their sensory impressions and to make sense out of their world. Mrs. Theoretical knew a lot about infants and toddlers and the kinds of things they are ready to learn. Her problem was that she had difficulty thinking about the kinds of activities that she could introduce to facilitate the infants' learning.

Please help Mrs. Theoretical by creating a simple activity that will foster an emerging skill.

1. By 2 months, the infant is beginning to put together information from different senses. She knows that if she hears a person's voice, she can look up and see that person, or if she hears the ringing of a rattle, she can find it with her eyes.

   Suggested activity to support this skill:

   _____

   _____

2. Between 3 and 4 months, the infant can anticipate when something that disappears will reappear and can reach out and grasp a toy.

   Suggested activity to support this skill:

   _____

   _____

3. Between 5 and 6 months, the infant is gaining a first awareness of cause and effect and will initiate activities that make interesting things happen.

   Suggested activity to support this skill:

   _____

   _____

4. Between 6 and 8 months, the infant is showing an increased interest in the properties of different objects, will transfer objects from one hand to the other, and will try out games like shaking and banging.

Suggested activity to support these skills:

_____

_____

5. Between 8 and 10 months, the infant comes to recognize that objects continue to exist even when they are out of sight.

Suggested activity to support this skill:

_____

_____

6. By 12 months and older, the infant shows interest in emptying, filling, and exploring boxes and containers.

Suggested activity to support these skills:

_____

_____

Even though they can't use words to describe what they are learning, infants and toddlers spend many of their waking hours manipulating toys and discovering how things work.

Complete the following paragraphs.

1. Cindy, at 5 months, was playing with a rubber duck. She discovered that:

_____

_____

2. Jerry, at 6 months, hit his bell toy and it made an interesting sound. He hit it again. He discovered that:

_____

_____

3. Madeline, at 9 months, was sitting on the floor, playing with a pan and a wooden spoon. She hit the pan with the spoon and discovered that:

_____

_____

4. Pedro, at 10 months, was playing Peek-a-Boo with his caregiver. He was discovering that:

_____

_____

To recognize expectable sequences in cognitive development in young toddlers and describe materials and activities that will enhance this development

You and your assistant teacher are taking care of six toddlers between 1 and 2 years of age. List one activity that would accomplish each of the following objectives.

1. To help the toddlers associate words with actions

_____

_____

2. To give the toddlers a chance to solve a problem

_____

_____

3. To encourage the toddlers to imitate actions and movements

_____

_____

Assume that you and your assistant are responsible for ten 2-year-olds. Design one activity that would accomplish each of the following objectives.

1. To allow the 2-year-olds to participate in and enjoy a circle activity

   _____

   _____

2. To give the 2-year-olds an opportunity to experiment with a new and interesting substance

   _____

   _____

3. To encourage the 2-year-olds to participate in a pretend activity

   _____

   _____

To recognize expectable sequences in cognitive development in older toddlers and describe materials and activities that will enhance this development

Between 2 and 3 years of age, the child first begins to learn about number and amount. He can tell the difference between *one* and *many* and begins to express this knowledge by using plurals when he talks about more than one thing. "Gimme cookie" becomes "Gimme cookies."

Alisha had been playing quietly in her own room while her mother was preparing dinner. Suddenly, her mother got worried. Alisha was not the sort of child who could play alone for more than two minutes. When she looked into Alisha's room, she was relieved to find Alisha perfectly fine, but the room was an absolute shambles. "What are you doing?" she asked Alisha. "Me packin'," Alisha explained as she pulled two bathing suits out of her drawer and added them to a huge pile of toys. Alisha's mother finally figured out what her daughter was doing. She was pretending that the family was going on a trip and was making a pile of all the things she wanted to take with her.

At 2 years old, children like Alisha are mastering a variety of sorting skills. They can go to the bookshelf and select the book they want to read, they can choose their favorite foods when they go grocery shopping, and they can be quite insistent about the clothes they want to wear on a particular day. Some 2-year-olds are able to sort by attributes such as color and size. They consistently select the biggest cookie or their favorite-colored lollipop.

Describe two sorting tasks that 2-year-olds are capable of mastering.

1. _____

_____

2. _____

_____

Number Skills

Mrs. Proud-Mom brought her son, Dedrick, to a new child care home. As she introduced Dedrick to his new child care provider, Mrs. Proud-Mom asked Dedrick to tell the child care provider how old he was. "Two," answered Dedrick quickly, holding up two fingers. "And now tell how old your sister is," prompted Mrs. Proud-Mom. "Three," Dedrick answered again, holding up the same two fingers.

At 2 years old, children like Dedrick are beginning to learn about numbers. They know the difference between *one* and *more than one* and are learning to recite numbers, or *count by rote.* Although 2-year-olds have not yet learned to count objects, they enjoy simple number rhymes and are able to put pairs of objects together, demonstrating an understanding of "twoness."

Describe one number rhyme that 2-year-olds enjoy and one game or action song that requires an understanding of two *or* more.

_____

_____

_____

_____

_____

Objective 4

To recognize expectable sequences in cognitive development in preschool children and describe materials and activities that will enhance this development

Developmental Sequences

The 3-year-old is beginning to learn that every object has certain features that describe it. Some of these features define the object, and some can change without changing the object. A person can change his hair color and still be the same person. If he becomes taller and heavier, he is still a person but no longer a child. An apple can be green or red and still be an apple, but it can never be an orange.

The 3-year-old loves taking things apart and putting them back together. By doing this, she comes to understand how different parts can go together to make a whole. At this age, playing with stacking toys, simple puzzles, blocks, and cars are favorite activities. If she has two sizes of things, she will call one "the big thing" and one "the small thing," but she cannot make comparisons and call one "bigger" or "smaller" than the other.

By 4, the child can choose the correct bottom half to go with the top half of a picture. He understands *back, over, under* and knows the relationships of rooms in his house to one another. He can tell how to get from one familiar place to another. For example, he knows how to get from his house to school. The 4-year-old can recognize likenesses and differences, and he is beginning to be able to make some comparisons. He is starting to understand the concepts of size (and to be able to use *bigger* and *smaller*) and of weight.

The 5-year-old becomes increasingly better at comparisons and relationships. She can look at a picture and tell if something is missing and can cut a picture into parts and put it back together. She can identify the biggest, longest, and smallest of three or four things and can tell you which thing is the middle and which is on top or in front.

The child is now aware of several different ways that objects can relate to each other. She can put together objects that belong in the bedroom, the kitchen, or the living room. She can associate a worker with the tools she uses, an animal with its house, and a mother animal with her baby. She can solve simple picture problems.

Describe three classroom activities that help a child learn about the attributes of or relationships among objects.

1. _____

2. _____

3. _____

Pattern Making

"Hmmm," Mrs. Green thought to herself. "It looks like Mrs. Wilson is going to be one of those nervous mothers." Mrs. Wilson was bringing her son in for a visit to the center. She stopped at the door to give a quick brush to a wisp of Jamie's hair, retied a straggly shoelace, and tucked in a corner of the shirt that had made its way out of Jamie's pants.

"I am glad you could make it. I am Mrs. Green, and I'll be Jamie's teacher. Jamie, would you like to play with this bead stacker while your mother and I talk for a little while?"

"I hope Jamie won't give you any trouble," Mrs. Wilson said. "He's a hard-headed boy. I have tried to teach him his colors, but he just doesn't get it."

During this conversation, Jamie took the posts out of the stacker, gathered up the beads, replaced the posts, and was putting the beads back on one of the posts—a red bead, a blue bead, a red bead, a blue bead. "Look what he's doing now," Mrs. Green exclaimed. "He's making color patterns with the beads."

Pattern making is a sophisticated skill that involves an orderly arrangement of elements. When a child alternates blue and red beads on a bead stacker, he is making a logical pattern. It is logical because once the pattern is started, you know what color comes next. When a child draws a self-portrait with two eyes, two ears, two arms, and two legs, he is making a symmetrical pattern. It is symmetrical because one side is a mirror image of the other.

At 3 years of age, children can begin to make logical patterns, but they can't hold on to their ideas. They may begin by making a paper chain of alternating blue and pink loops, but after four or five loops, they may get interested in making all the loops big and forget about alternating the colors.

At 4 years of age, most children can make a logical pattern by alternating two elements but will have difficulty with a three-element pattern, such as red-yellow-blue, red-yellow-blue. A second skill that children achieve by 4 years old is making a simple symmetrical pattern. They can make a square house with a door in the middle and a window on each side.

By 5 years of age, children become adept at pattern making. They can make logical patterns with three or four elements and symmetrical patterns like palm trees and Valentine hearts. They can also make matrix patterns involving double classification. If you remove one element of the matrix, the 5-year-old will tell you the color and shape of the missing element.

Number Skills

At 3 years of age, most children have a good understanding of *one* and *two*. They will join in finger play, putting up one finger and then two fingers. With practice and experience, they will count up to three fingers and three objects.

The 4-year-old recites her numbers up to 10 and counts objects up to 4. She is ready to learn one-to-one correspondence. This means that she is ready to put down one new object for each object that is already down—one hat for each doll or one driver for each truck. Because she is just learning this skill, she does it easily with objects that are familiar and go naturally together. It is easy for her to give one hat to each doll. It is harder for her to give one cantaloupe to each dragonfly.

The 5-year-old can count at least up to 13 but only knows his numbers because of memorization. He does not understand number concepts beyond the number 5, and so his number experiences should be concerned with small numbers taught with concrete objects. By now, he is able to match number sets, such as three elephants with three tigers and two horses with two cows. If he has had an opportunity to learn them, he can name the numerals and put together sets of numerals up to 5. If you put down a card with the numeral 5, the 5-year-old can place 5 beads next to it.

Describe three classroom activities that help a child learn numerical relationships.

1. _____

2. _____

3. _____

Sammy is playing with two trucks—one is a red truck about 2 inches high and one is a blue truck about 4 inches high. Sammy calls the red truck "the little truck." He races his trucks across the room and declares loudly, "The big truck won!" "I gots the big truck!" his friend Violette shouts. She knocks down Sammy's blue truck with her dump truck. Sammy rescues his red truck without putting up an argument. It's just as well that he didn't. Violette understands *big* and *small,* but she is too young to understand that Sammy called the blue truck "big" because it was bigger than the red truck, even though it was smaller than her dump truck. As Violette and Sammy gain experience with words as well as objects, they learn to make comparisons and discover many different kinds of spatial relationships that describe their physical world.

To learn how to create a preschool environment that encourages exploration, curiosity, and critical thinking

Mrs. No-Nonsense wanted to teach her preschool class about different kinds of measurement. For their first lesson, she brought in a yardstick, a small scale, and a thermometer. "This is a thermometer," she explained in circle time. "It tells us how hot something is. This is a scale. It tells us how much something weighs. This is a yardstick. We use it to measure length. Do you all understand? Now, I have a question for you. If I want to know how tall Bobby is, would I use a yardstick, a thermometer, or a scale?"

"I know, I know!" Wilson responded, waving his hand in the air. "You would use a scale 'cause that is what is in the doctor's office."

Before Mrs. No-Nonsense could respond, Becky shouted out, "I got another idea! You could ask his mommy when she picks him up after school."

Poor Mrs. No-Nonsense. No matter how hard she tried, she couldn't teach the children about the different kinds of measurement. One problem was that she was trying to teach a concept that was much too abstract. A second problem was that she didn't have a real understanding about how children learn.

Children are naturally curious. From the moment of birth, they actively seek out information and search for patterns and consistencies. As children grow older, they are able to remember these past experiences and explorations and use the old information to make sense out of the new.

Teachers who are concerned with children's learning must take advantage of their inborn curiosity and natural excitement about learning. Instead of trying to teach children abstract concepts and disconnected facts, like Mrs. No-Nonsense, teachers need to increase children's opportunities to explore, experiment, and discover. They need to provide children with new and exciting materials and experiences, ask children open-ended questions that encourage speculation, encourage children to carry out experiments and generate questions, and provide children with opportunities to create and solve their own problems.

Help Mrs. No-Nonsense come up with four age-appropriate topics for her classroom, where the children are able to conduct their own hands-on experiments.

1. _____
2. _____
3. _____
4. _____

Ask Open-Ended Questions That Encourage Speculation

Despite her best efforts, Mrs. No-Nonsense was not happy with the do-it-yourself approach to science. The next day in circle time, she planned a series of questions on growing things to make sure that the children were learning. Here is her list of questions:

Do seeds grow into plants?

Do plants need water?

Do plants need sun?

Just as Mrs. No-Nonsense was about to begin circle time, she was called to use the phone and Mrs. Fun took over. Mrs. Fun decided to change the three questions from closed to open-ended questions, so that children would have a chance to speculate. She began with, "What do you thimk would happen if I soaked the little seed in water and then very carefully put some dirt in the pot, put in the seed, and covered it with more dirt?"

Help Mrs. No-Nonsense rephrase her three questions to spark curiosity and encourage speculation.

1. _____
2. _____
3. _____

Encourage Children to Ask Questions on Their Own

At the end of the week, Mrs. No-Nonsense was standing near the science area. Terry asked her if the plants could learn to walk.

"That's a dumb question," Mrs. No-Nonsense insisted. "Of course plants can't walk!"

Obviously, Mrs. No-Nonsense's answer was insulting, and Terry was not likely to ask another question.

How could Mrs. No-Nonsense have responded to Terry?

_____

_____

_____

Encourage Problem Solving

Mrs. No-Nonsense still needs your help. Now, she is preparing a science lesson on frogs. She has pulled out two activities that she and her assistant developed last year:

Activity 1: Show the children pictures of the life cycle of a frog using a "big book." Make sure that the children learn to identify the eggs, the tadpoles, and the mature frogs. Divide the children into groups, and give each group a set of sequence cards showing the life cycle of the frog. See which group is the first to line up the cards in the correct sequence.

Activity 2: Fill a fishbowl with water from a pond with live tadpoles in it. Leave it in the science area and encourage the children to watch the tadpoles. At circle time, ask the children "What did you wonder about when you looked at the fishbowl?" If no one says anything, get the conversation going yourself. For example, try "I wonder what we should feed the tadpoles?" or "I wonder how long it takes for a tadpole to turn into a frog?"

Which activity should Mrs. No-Nonsense use if she wants the children to carry out experiments and engage in problem solving?

Activity # _____

Reward Children's Natural Curiosity by Responding to It

What are some of the questions that preschool children typically ask in the science corner?

1. _____

2. _____

3. _____

In the art area?

1. _____

2. _____

3. _____

Identify three activities you have recently used that elicited questions from your children.

1. _____

2. _____

3. _____

Provide New Information and Experiences

Children enjoy exploring new materials, but it is important to select materials carefully and not to overwhelm children by providing too much at once.

- *Selection of materials:* When choosing materials for display and use, be guided by the number of children using the area at one time, the size of the storage facilities, and the need to satisfy the range of abilities of the children in the class. Also remember to rotate the toys and materials periodically.
- *Variety of materials:* Provide a variety of materials that appeal to different senses. A good classroom will contain some interesting things to touch, taste, and smell as well as to look at and listen to.

In the space below, list five things that aren't ordinarily considered classroom materials but that can be used to stimulate the senses in a classroom situation. (Remember that snacktime can be made interesting, too.)

1. _____

2. _____

3. _____

4. _____

5. _____

To learn techniques for introducing meaningful themes into preschool classrooms

The more familiar we are with a particular concept or area of knowledge, the harder it is for us to recognize how much a young child must learn. Think about all the questions a small child might ask about a simple trip to the grocery store:

Why do we need money to go the grocery store?

Where did the money come from?

How do we decide what to buy at the supermarket?

Do we decide before we go to the grocery store what we need?

How do we know what we need?

When we go into the store, how do we know where to find the things on our list?

Why is some food put in the refrigerator?

Why do we give the cashier money? What does she do with it?

Why does she give us money back?

As we realize how much a child can learn about everyday events, we recognize that themes upon which to build a curriculum are at our fingertips. The young child lives in the here and now. He must become familiar with the aspects of living he confronts on a daily basis before he can learn about things that are remote in either space or time.

List four themes that can be used in the preschool classroom that are based on everyday experiences. (Be sure the themes include enough concepts to keep the children interested for several days.)

1. _____

2. _____

3. _____

4. _____

Mrs. Creativity-Minus selected a new theme for the second month of preschool. She decided that it would be a good idea to teach the children about weather. She wrote up three plans for activities that would focus on the weather:

Activity 1

Objective: Teach the children how to spell *weather*.

Procedure: Give each child the seven letters that spell the word *weather*. Write the word *weather* on the chalkboard. Ask each child to find a seat at a table and arrange her letters in the correct order so that they will spell the word *weather*.

Activity 2

Objective: Teach the children how to count objects up to 10 using one-to-one correspondence.

Procedure: Gather a large bunch of leaves from the playground. Count out 10 leaves for each child. Ask each child to count the leaves. Let all of the children who can count to 10 stand in front of the class and show the other children how to count to 10.

Activity 3

Objective: Teach the children how to write a sentence.

Procedure: Write this sentence on the chalkboard: *I love to play with leaves.* Give each child a pencil and a sheet of paper. Ask him to write the sentence on one side of the paper and to draw a picture on the other side.

Mrs. Creativity-Minus needs your help. Using Weather as the theme, develop three different activities that will help the children learn about weather in a meaningful way.

1. _____

2. _____

3. _____

COGNITIVE • *Observation Opportunities*

Name _____

Observation Opportunity 1

Observe an infant one or more times, and then complete the following checklist.

	Yes	No	Not Observed	Describe Activity
The infant is able to coordinate what she sees and hears.	☐	☐	☐	_____ _____
The infant tries to make interesting things happen again.	☐	☐	☐	_____ _____
The infant looks at herself in the mirror.	☐	☐	☐	_____ _____
The infant recognizes that objects still exist even when they are out of sight.	☐	☐	☐	_____ _____
The infant is able to grasp an object.	☐	☐	☐	_____ _____
The infant switches an object from one hand to the other.	☐	☐	☐	_____ _____
The infant plays with different toys in different ways.	☐	☐	☐	_____ _____

Observation Opportunity 2

Observe a toddler one or more times, and then complete the following checklist.

	Yes	No	Not Observed	Describe Activity
The toddler sorts according to color.	☐	☐	☐	_____ _____
The toddler uses one finger to point to an object.	☐	☐	☐	_____ _____
The toddler empties and fills a container.	☐	☐	☐	_____ _____
The toddler places one block on top of another.	☐	☐	☐	_____ _____
The toddler finds a matching object.	☐	☐	☐	_____ _____
The toddler recognizes herself in the mirror.	☐	☐	☐	_____ _____
The toddler completes a two- to five-piece knobbed puzzle.	☐	☐	☐	_____ _____
The toddler imitates actions.	☐	☐	☐	_____ _____
The toddler shows early signs of pretending.	☐	☐	☐	_____ _____

Observation Opportunity 3

Observe a preschooler one or more times, and then complete the following checklist.

	Yes	No	Not Observed	Describe Activity
The child sorts according to size.	☐	☐	☐	_____ _____
The child sorts according to number.	☐	☐	☐	_____ _____
The child uses blocks to represent a real-world building, road, or other structure.	☐	☐	☐	_____ _____
The child stacks blocks.	☐	☐	☐	_____ _____
The child stabilizes a structure by putting larger blocks on the bottom.	☐	☐	☐	_____ _____
The child creates a symmetrical pattern.	☐	☐	☐	_____ _____
The child shows pattern making with the blocks.	☐	☐	☐	_____ _____

COGNITIVE • Challenge Activities

Name _____

Challenge 1

Create, carry out, and evaluate three cognitive activities using but not limited to such recycled items as paper towel tubes, plastic milk bottle tops, shells, empty boxes, meat trays, old calendars, egg cartons, old greeting cards, and keys. Use the following activity sheet to describe each of the activities.

Activity 1: _____

Age Group: _____

Description: What are you going to do?

_____

_____

_____

Objective: What will the children learn from this?

_____

_____

_____

Materials Used:

_____

_____

Procedures: How will you carry out this activity?

_____

_____

Evaluation: Did the activity turn out the way you planned? What changes would you make the next time you do this activity?

_____

_____

Activity 2: _____

Age Group: _____

Description: What are you going to do?

_____

_____

_____

_____

Objective: What will the children learn from this?

_____

_____

_____

_____

Materials Used:

_____

_____

Procedures: How will you carry out this activity?

_____

_____

_____

_____

Evaluation: Did the activity turn out the way you planned? What changes would you make the next time you do this activity?

_____

_____

_____

Activity 3: _____

Age Group: _____

Description: What are you going to do?

_____

_____

_____

_____

Objective: What will the children learn from this?

_____

_____

_____

_____

Materials Used:

_____

_____

Procedures: How will you carry out this activity?

_____

_____

_____

_____

Evaluation: Did the activity turn out the way you planned? What changes would you make the next time you do this activity?

_____

_____

_____

Challenge 2

Describe, carry out, and evaluate three science/discovery activities appropriate for your age group.

Activity 1: _____

Age Group: _____

Description: What are you going to do?

_____

_____

_____

_____

Objective: What will the children learn from this?

_____

_____

_____

Materials Used:

_____

_____

Procedures: How will you carry out this activity?

_____

_____

_____

Evaluation: Did the activity turn out the way you planned? What changes would you make the next time you do this activity?

_____

_____

_____

Activity 2: _____

Age Group: _____

Description: What are you going to do?

_____

_____

_____

_____

Objective: What will the children learn from this?

_____

_____

_____

_____

Materials Used:

_____

_____

Procedures: How will you carry out this activity?

_____

_____

_____

_____

Evaluation: Did the activity turn out the way you planned? What changes would you make the next time you do this activity?

_____

_____

_____

Activity 3: _____

Age Group: _____

Description: What are you going to do?

_____

_____

_____

_____

Objective: What will the children learn from this?

_____

_____

_____

_____

Materials Used:

_____

_____

Procedures: How will you carry out this activity?

_____

_____

_____

_____

Evaluation: Did the activity turn out the way you planned? What changes would you make the next time you do this activity?

_____

_____

_____

● COGNITIVE ● Post-Training Wrap-Up

After completing this unit, review your personal goal and action plan from the beginning of the unit and describe how you accomplished your goal.

_____

_____

_____

_____

List at least three ways in which you changed your behavior as a result of your training in this Functional Area.

1. _____

2. _____

3. _____

● COGNITIVE ● Professional Resource File

Resource Items

Collect the items for the Professional Resource File related to this Functional Area (if applicable). Refer to the pages at the back of this *Trainee's Manual* (pp. 281–283) and to the CDA booklet from the Council for Professional Recognition for specific instructions.

Statement of Competence

Write a short essay of 75 to 150 words, listing one or more goals you have for promoting children's cognitive development and describing the activities you do to achieve these goals. Describe your experiences in your own words. Be concise. Use "I" statements—for example, "I provide a variety of materials for children to explore as they play. I encourage children to explore items that seem interesting."

For additional information about writing your Statement of Competence, refer to the workbook section at the end of this *Trainee's Manual* (pp. 283–312) and to the CDA booklet from the Council for Professional Recognition.

Competency Goal II
To advance physical and intellectual competence

Chapter 6

Communication

Overview

Communication is the sharing of thoughts, feelings, and ideas through language or through nonverbal means, such as gestures, facial expressions, and art.

Rationale

Language, a uniquely human accomplishment, is the basis of much of our thinking as well as our communication. It is the primary way we receive the accumulated wisdom of humankind and communicate with people remote to us in space and time. Language is also the way we communicate with ourselves, recalling past events, working out problems, planning ahead, and keeping our impulses in check. We urge children to think before they act, just as we urge children to "use their words" to control the behaviors of others.

We think about school as the time when children learn reading, writing, and arithmetic. We can think about preschool as the time when children develop the language skills underlying these school-related achievements. Language development begins at birth, as the baby and her caregivers communicate with gaze, sound, and touch. Teachers and caregivers provide children with many opportunities to learn communication skills, to use verbal and nonverbal means to communicate their own ideas and feelings, and to understand the ideas and feelings of others.

Objectives

- **Objective 1**   To recognize the relationship between language development and real-world experiences

- **Objective 2**   To describe the expectable sequence of communication skills in infants and suggest ways to support their development

- **Objective 3**   To describe the expectable sequence of communication skills in young toddlers and suggest ways to support their development

- **Objective 4**   To describe the expectable sequence of language skills in older toddlers and suggest ways to support their development

- **Objective 5**   To describe the expectable sequence of language skills in preschool children and suggest ways to support their development

- **Objective 6**   To learn ways of reading to children that encourage active participation and engender a love of books

- **Objective 7**   To describe early literacy skills and suggest activities that promote them

- **Objective 8**   To describe the small-muscle skills that are used in writing and suggest activities that develop these skills and provide children with opportunities to practice writing

- **Objective 9**   To select books that foster empathy, promote prosocial behavior, counteract bias, and support bilingualism

COMMUNICATION • Pretest

Answer True (T) or False (F) for each of the following statements.

_____ 1. It is good to correct a 4-year-old's grammar.

_____ 2. Children who cannot pronounce all sounds by the time they are 4 years old should be referred to speech therapy.

_____ 3. Children should be encouraged to ask questions.

_____ 4. There is no relationship between imaginative play and language development.

_____ 5. Children should never be made to feel that the language spoken in their home is in any way inferior.

_____ 6. It is silly to talk to an infant under 6 months.

_____ 7. Cooing, babbling, and gesturing are important prelanguage skills.

List three things to consider when reading a book to a group of 3- to 5-year-olds.

1. _____

_____

2. _____

_____

3. _____

_____

COMMUNICATION • Self-Assessment

Indicate how you feel about your skills and abilities in each of the following categories by checking the appropriate column.

	Pretraining		
	Strong	**Satisfactory**	**Needs Improvement**
I recognize the relationship between language development and real-world experiences.	☐	☐	☐
I can describe the expectable sequence of communication skills in infants and suggest ways to support their development.	☐	☐	☐
I can describe the expectable sequence of communication skills in young toddlers and suggest ways to support their development.	☐	☐	☐
I can describe the expectable sequence of language skills in older toddlers and suggest ways to support their development.	☐	☐	☐
I can describe the expectable sequence of language skills in preschool children and suggest ways to support their development.	☐	☐	☐
I know ways of reading to children that encourage active participation and engender a love of books.	☐	☐	☐
I can describe early literacy skills and suggest activities that promote them.	☐	☐	☐
I can describe the small-muscle skills that are used in writing and suggest activities that develop these skills and provide children with opportunities to practice writing.	☐	☐	☐
I can select books that foster empathy, promote prosocial behavior, counteract bias, and support bilingualism.	☐	☐	☐

COMMUNICATION • Pretraining Personal Goal

Based on your pretraining self-assessment, write a personal goal for this Functional Area and an action plan describing how you will accomplish the goal.

Goal _____

_____

_____

_____

Action Plan _____

_____

_____

_____

_____

_____

_____

_____

_____

_____

_____

_____

Save your goal and action plan for the end of this unit so you will be able to answer these questions: How did you accomplish your goal? And how has your behavior changed based on your training?

To recognize the relationship between language development and real-world experiences

Children cannot talk about things unless they experience them. The more direct experiences children have, the more they have to talk about. Even the simple nouns and adjectives that children use in everyday language have meanings based on real experiences. The child cannot know the meaning of *soft* unless she has experienced both hard and soft. She cannot know the meaning of *smooth* unless she experiences both rough and smooth.

List 20 new vocabulary words that can be introduced on the ride or walk to the child care setting.

_____	_____
_____	_____
_____	_____
_____	_____
_____	_____
_____	_____
_____	_____
_____	_____
_____	_____
_____	_____

"You know," Mrs. Kirk explained, "my Susie doesn't talk. She's a bright girl, but she doesn't talk." Susie's mother didn't do much talking either, and no matter how hard Mrs. Bartley, the child care teacher, tried, she could not get any more information from her about 3-year-old Susie.

"Susie," Mrs. Bartley suggested, "would you like to come and sit in the circle with the other children?" Susie said "Uh" and followed Mrs. Bartley to the circle.

It was a busy morning, and Mrs. Bartley didn't have a lot of time to spend with Susie. Except for the fact that Susie didn't talk, she seemed to get along fine with the rest of the children. She joined in a game of kick-and-chase-the-ball on the playground. She helped create a giant sandcastle in the beach corner. She even took her turn with easel painting, as if she had been in school for a long time.

At snacktime, she had problems opening her milk carton. "Would you like some help?" Mrs. Bartley asked. "Uh," said Susie, holding up the container. At storytime, Susie worked her way up to the front of the class. She looked at the pictures as Mrs. Bartley read the story *Rainbow Fish* and looked quite concerned when Rainbow Fish only had one scale left. "Would you like to bring your painting home to Mommy?" Mrs. Bartley asked Susie at closing time. "Uh," said Susie, and she ran to her cubby to gather up her paper.

Which statement is true about Susie?

_____ Susie is developmentally delayed.

_____ Susie is a bright girl but is delayed in language development.

_____ Susie's language output is minimal but her receptive language is age appropriate.

_____ Susie has an emotional problem.

As we realize from the story of Susie, the number of words a child says does not necessarily reflect the amount of language she knows. Some children seem to be uneven in language development. Although they are slow about speaking, they attend to spoken language and are able to understand what they hear. Fortunately, children with normal hearing who understand language are almost certain to learn speech. Therefore, the critical role of the teacher in encouraging language development is to provide children with opportunities to hear language spoken in a meaningful context.

To describe the expectable sequence of communication skills in infants and suggest ways to support their development

Alicia and her friend were watching their neighbor, a teenage mother, wheeling her baby through the supermarket. Every few minutes, she would stop and talk to her baby. The baby would babble to her and she would babble back, just as if they were carrying on a real conversation.

"She's so silly," Alicia remarked. "That baby is too young to talk. You would think she'd be embarrassed." Alicia's friend disagreed. "I don't see anything silly about talking to a baby. Look at how well the baby responds, and besides, she is learning something. She's learning to tune into language, taking turns in a back-and-forth conversation."

Alicia's friend was right, of course. Children begin to learn language in infancy, and mothers and other caregivers who talk to and read to their babies are giving them a sound foundation for learning language.

Here are some concerns that parents have expressed about their children's language development. Using your text as a guide, respond to these concerns.

Natasha is 3 months old. She makes different vowel sounds, like "oo" and "ee," but I can't get her to make any consonant sounds. When I say "Ma-ma," she says "ah-ah," and when I say "Da-da," she says "aa-aa." How can I help her learn to say "Da-da"? It would make her dad so happy.

_____

_____

Pedro is 7 months old, and before he falls asleep and as soon as he awakens, he starts saying "Da-da, Da-da, Da-da." I don't know whether he is saying "Da-da" just because he likes playing with sounds or if it's because he wants his daddy to come in. I wish he would learn to say "Ma-ma." What should I be doing?

_____

_____

When my husband and I talk to each other, we just naturally talk in Spanish, but recently Alphonso, our 9-month-old, has started to babble. What worries me is that when he babbles, he sounds as if he is saying nonsense words in Spanish. I really want him to learn English. It will be much easier for him when he gets to school. Do you think that my husband and I should switch to English when we talk in front of Alphonso?

_____

_____

My Bartholomew is 10 months old. When I say "No," he stops and looks at me and then goes right ahead and does whatever he wants. Is he slow with understanding language?

_____

_____

As we look at the kinds of questions parents have been asking, it is obvious that some parents as well as some caregivers could benefit from a list of suggestions for fostering language development in the first year of life. Complete the following sentences.

When a baby is between birth and 3 months, it is important to establish communication by:

_____

_____

Between 3 and 6 months, it is important to expose a baby to the sounds of language by:

_____

_____

Language activities that babies between 6 and 9 months enjoy include:

_____

_____

Language activities that help a 9- to 14-month-old infant understand the meanings of words include:

_____

_____

To describe the expectable sequence of communication skills in young toddlers and suggest ways to support their development

You will notice that young toddlers acquire language skills at different rates and in different ways. While most young toddlers acquire five or six meaningful words by 14 months old, other toddlers who understand the meanings of words don't begin to say more than one or two words until they are 2 or 2½ years old. Still other young toddlers have an extensive one-word vocabulary and may even be talking in two- or three-word sentences by the time they are 24 months.

There is also a wide range of difference in the timetable for developing receptive language (understanding spoken language), and we should not expect that same-age toddlers have the same level of understanding. At the same time, if parents describe language concerns that are out of the ordinary, it is a good idea to suggest evaluation by a developmental specialist.

Responding to Parental Concerns

As you respond to the parents in this exercise, try to sort out the differences that are in the broad range of normal from the differences that indicate a delay and may be a cause for concern.

Hannah is 14 months old. I'm worried about her language. She seems to understand what I say to her. When I tell her to show me her tummy, she'll pick up her shirt and point to it, or if I ask her to find *Goodnight Moon*, she'll go right to the shelf and get it. The problem is that she has a very small vocabulary. At this age, her older sister had a really good vocabulary and was even putting two or three words together. The only words Hannah can say are "Nana," which can mean *grandma* or *banana*, "Baba" meaning *bottle*, and "Dada," "car," and "doggie." I can't even get her to say "Mommy." Should I have her tested?

_____

_____

My mother is constantly bugging me about Daryl. He's only 18 months old, and she keeps telling me that I should take him to the doctor because he hasn't started talking. I keep telling her to stop worrying. Daryl understands language fine. When I tell him to play Patty-Cake, he claps, and when I tell him to say "bye-bye," he waves. He babbles all the time, but he doesn't say words that you can understand. I keep telling my mother that boys are slower than girls about starting to talk and that he will talk when he's ready. Einstein didn't start talking until he was 5 years old. How can I convince my mother that there's nothing wrong with Daryl?

_____

_____

Bobbie is 20 months old. He has great motor skills and he's good at doing puzzles and stacking his blocks, but he's really behind in language. He knows about 30 words and that's it. He never puts two words together, except for

"My ball" and "My truck." My husband keeps telling me he's fine, but I do feel that it's time to start worrying. What do you think?

_____

_____

Mrs. Tight-Lips is very sweet and loving with children, but she hardly ever talks to them. Parents often complain that she doesn't do anything with the children to encourage language. Please provide Mrs. Tight-Lips with a list of five activities that will help young toddlers develop receptive and/or expressive language.

1. _____

2. _____

3. _____

4. _____

5. _____

Objective 4

To describe the expectable sequence of language skills in older toddlers and suggest ways to support their development

Respond to the following parent queries.

Marlena is 2 years old. Her grammar is terrible. She says things like "Daddy home car" and "More cookie me." How can I help her?

_____

_____

Honey is 2½ years old. She is a beautiful little girl. The only problem with her is that we can't get her to talk. I know she can talk because she was already saying words when she was 14 months old. She used to say "Daddy," "Mommy," "Bendy" (that's our dog's name), "hot," "no," and lots of other words that I can't remember. How can I convince her to start talking?

_____

_____

Anthony is a real chatter-box, and he can talk your ear off. The problem is that even though my husband and I are very careful about speaking correctly in front of him, he keeps making ridiculous mistakes. The other day, I wrote down some of his sentences. Here they are: "I bited my apple." "I sawed two mouses." "I eated all my dinner." Anthony is almost 3 years old. Shouldn't he be speaking correctly by now?

_____

_____

Describe one activity that will help older toddlers expand their vocabulary and one activity that will help older toddlers learn to follow directions.

1. _____

2. _____

Objective 5

To describe the expectable sequence of language skills in preschool children and suggest ways to support their development

Respond to the following questions that parents asked during a parent/teacher meeting.

Pedro is 4½ years old, and he can talk up a storm. The problem is that people are always complaining that they don't understand him. I never have a problem. I understand every word he says. The teacher in his preschool suggested that I take him to the clinic, where they do some sort of language screening test. Should I listen to her?

_____

_____

Amanda is 4½, and she is driving us crazy. She is always asking questions, and even if we have already answered the question, she'll ask the same question again. "Where does the sun go when it's night time?" "How does Santa Claus get down the chimney?" "How come dogs don't have hands like monkeys?" "What happens to the wind when it stops blowing?" Is there something the matter with Amanda's memory, or is she just being a pest?

_____

_____

Angelica is almost 5 years old. Her talking is pretty good, but she has trouble pronouncing some words. She still calls *Massachusetts* "Massatusetts," and she sometimes says "pasghetti" instead of *spaghetti.* Should I have her hearing tested?

_____

_____

To learn ways of reading to children that encourage active participation and engender a love for books

"My son won't listen to stories," Mr. Darrell complained. "I have the most beautiful collection of fairy tales—a whole big volume—and he shows no interest at all. The only thing he wants to do is look at the pictures."

"I'm not surprised that he enjoys the pictures," Mrs. Smith commented. "All the children at school love pictures. I always try to choose stories that have interesting pictures to go with every page. I've even learned to read upside down so that the children can look at the pictures while I read."

"Sounds to me as if they're wasting time with the pictures instead of reading the story," Mr. Darrell said. "You know what's going to happen? When they get to school, they'll be guessing what it says from the pictures instead of reading the words."

To that, Mrs. Smith replied, "It's true that some children are quite talented at picture interpretation. It's one of the skills children develop as they simultaneously listen to words and look at pictures. The wonderful thing about it is that children who read pictures really do feel as if they are reading."

Mr. Darrell was still unsatisfied. "Sounds as if we're teaching children to become pretend readers."

"I guess you could say that. And you can also be sure that children who enjoy pretend reading will also enjoy real reading, especially if we introduce books that are meaningful for them."

"What do you mean by *meaningful?*" Mr. Darrell asked.

"I think of a book as meaningful," Mrs. Smith began, "if the children can relate to the characters and develop feeling for them. Our group has certain books they really love—books about animals, books about babies—Oh, I could go on and on."

"I know you could do that all right, but you still haven't answered my question," replied Mr. Darrell. "Why doesn't my son enjoy reading?"

Give five suggestions to Mr. Darrell for how to increase his son's interest in books.

1. _____

2. _____

3. _____

4. _____

5. _____

Reading Stories

Reading stories to children can be the highlight of the day for both the teacher and the children, or it can be a complete disaster for everyone.

In order to make story reading a good experience, we have to give serious thought to all aspects of reading stories:

1. Selection of books
2. Selection of a reading setting
3. Appropriate ways of reading to children
4. Appropriate ways of integrating the stories with the classroom curriculum and the children's home experiences

Selecting Books

We could begin this section by giving you a list of the best books for young children, but that would create two problems. In the first place, what's right for most children may not be right for your children. In the second place, the list of best books today may not be tomorrow's best list.

The solution, of course, is for you to develop your own criteria for selecting books to read to your class.

Begin by listing the 10 books that the children in your group enjoy most.

1. _____

2. _____

3. _____

4. _____

5. _____

6. _____

7. _____

8. _____

9. _____

10. _____

Read the books with the children and answer these questions.

1. What illustrations in the books do the children enjoy?

   _____

2. How are the books culturally sensitive and appropriate?

   _____

3. What kinds of things make the children laugh?

   _____

4. What parts of the stories do the children want repeated?

   _____

5. What parts of the stories encourage the children to ask questions and make comments?

   _____

6. How long are the books the children enjoy?

   _____

7. Who are their favorite characters?

   _____

Now you are ready to develop your own selection criteria for the age group you work with.

Appropriate themes are:

_____

_____

Competency Goal II • To advance physical and intellectual competence

A good length is between:

_____

The storyline should:

_____

The illustrations should:

_____

The characters should be:

_____

Humor should:

_____

Objective 7

To describe early literacy skills and suggest activities that promote them

Mrs. Knucklehead came into the director's office in a huff. Her neighbor's child had come home from preschool with a page of A's she had copied and then recited the whole alphabet for her mother. "As far as I can tell, all the kids in *this* school do is play. I want my child to learn how to read. What are you going to do about it?"

The director explained that there were different philosophies about the best way to teach literacy. Every day in her school, the teachers engage the children in at least eight activities that prepare them to read and write.

Help this preschool director explain to Mrs. Knucklehead how children learn literacy skills in an age-appropriate manner. Complete this list of early literacy activities.

In order to build children's vocabulary, we:

_____

_____

_____

We engage the children in shared reading activities as a way to:

_____

_____

We introduce children to the sounds of letters by:

_____

_____

We immerse children in a print-rich environment by:

_____

_____

Our pretend play activities provide children with the opportunity to:

_____

_____

We have discovered that when children make their own books, they:

_____

_____

To describe the small-muscle skills that are used in writing and suggest activities that develop these skills and provide children with opportunities to practice writing

Using an instrument to write letters and words is a complex skill. The child needs to develop the dexterity to hold a pencil firmly between her thumb and first two fingers and at the same time swivel her wrist in order to form a letter. In order to keep her letters on a horizontal row, she needs to coordinate the movement of her hand and the movement of her eyes.

When Mrs. Clueless was asked to order materials that could help her 3-year-olds get ready for writing, she came up with the following list: ballpoint pens, lined loose-leaf notebook paper, letter stencils, ink erasers, writing pads, magnetic letters, and alphabet blocks.

Before her director sees the list, please revise it by substituting five items that will be better for 3-year-olds.

1. _____

2. _____

3. _____

4. _____

5. _____

Mrs. Clueless is grateful for your help, but she is still in trouble. Her director asked her why *she selected the five items you substituted and she doesn't have a clue. She needs your help again. Please explain each one.*

1. _____

2. _____

3. _____

4. _____

5. _____

Objective 9 — To select books that foster empathy, promote prosocial behavior, counteract bias, and support bilingualism

Mrs. Super-Careful had just opened a family child care home and already had four children enrolled. She had a 2-year-old who was African American, a 3-year-old who was described by his mother as "aggressive," a 4-year-old who was in the custody of his grandmother, and a 5-year-old from a Latino family who spoke mostly Spanish.

Select one book for each child that Mrs. Super-Careful could find at the library and describe the rationale for your selection.

1. _____

2. _____

3. _____

4. _____

COMMUNICATION • Observation Opportunities

Name _____

Observation Opportunity 1

Observe an infant one or more times with a caregiver. Complete the following checklist.

	Yes	No	Comments
The infant turns to the source of sound.	☐	☐	_____
The infant engages in back-and-forth conversation.	☐	☐	_____
The infant engages in vocal play.	☐	☐	_____
The infant babbles using consonants— e.g., "Da-da," "ba-ba," "Ma-ma."	☐	☐	_____
The infant follows two to three commands —e.g., "Wave bye-bye," "Play Patty-Cake."	☐	☐	_____
The infant engages in expressive jargon (uses strings of babble that sound like a sentence).	☐	☐	_____
The infant recognizes the parent's or caregiver's voice.	☐	☐	_____
The infant uses gestures as a way of communicating.	☐	☐	_____

Observation Opportunity 2

Observe a toddler several times, if needed, and complete the following checklist.

	Yes	No	**List Words (if applicable or possible)**
The toddler names at least five toys.	☐	☐	_____ _____
The toddler identifies at least 10 common toys or objects by pointing to or going toward an object when named.	☐	☐	_____ _____
The toddler enjoys playing with words—e.g., making up a nonsense rhyme.	☐	☐	_____ _____
The toddler pays attention when an adult reads a simple book.	☐	☐	_____ _____
The toddler puts two words together to make his wants known or to comment on something interesting—e.g., "baby book" means baby wants the book or the book belongs to baby; "Daddy hat" can mean Daddy is wearing a hat or that the hat belongs to Daddy.	☐	☐	_____ _____ _____ _____
The toddler is able to use sentences with three to five words.	☐	☐	_____ _____
The toddler has a spontaneous vocabulary of at least 10 ☐ 20 ☐ 50 ☐ or 100 ☐ words (check one).	☐	☐	_____ _____

Observation Opportunity 3

Observe a preschool class for 15 minutes during circle time. Describe the different functions of language used by children by completing the following chart.

Questions asked by a child:

_____

_____

Questions answered by a child:

_____

_____

Language used by a child describing an event or object:

_____

_____

_____

Language used by a child to explain:

_____

_____

_____

Language used by a child playfully:

_____

_____

_____

Language used by a child to refer to the future:

_____

_____

_____

● COMMUNICATION ● Challenge Activities

Name _____

Challenge 1

Describe three children's books appropriate for your age group. Fill out the following forms explaining why you have selected each book.

Title of Book 1: _____

Author: _____

Illustrator: _____

Publisher: _____   Date published: _____

Age group that would enjoy this book:

_____

Type of book:

_____

How does the book check out for antibias themes?

_____

_____

Describe the illustrations. How do they capture the children's attention?

_____

_____

_____

What techniques would you use to encourage participation from the children?

_____

_____

_____

Title of Book 2: _____

Author: _____

Illustrator: _____

Publisher: _____   Date published: _____

Age group that would enjoy this book:

_____

Type of book:

_____

How does the book check out for antibias themes?

_____

_____

_____

Describe the illustrations. How do they capture the children's attention?

_____

_____

_____

_____

_____

What techniques would you use to encourage participation from the children?

_____

_____

_____

_____

_____

Title of Book 3: _____

Author: _____

Illustrator: _____

Publisher: _____   Date published: _____

Age group that would enjoy this book:

_____

Type of book:

_____

How does the book check out for antibias themes?

_____

_____

_____

Describe the illustrations. How do they capture the children's attention?

_____

_____

_____

_____

_____

What techniques would you use to encourage participation from the children?

_____

_____

_____

_____

_____

Challenge 2

Create a book for the children in your age group, or have the children help you create a book for the classroom.

Title of your book: _____

Age group: _____

What is your book about?

_____

_____

_____

_____

_____

_____

How will you use this book?

_____

_____

_____

_____

_____

_____

Describe how you created your book.

_____

_____

_____

_____

_____

_____

Challenge 3

Develop a literature experience that you could share with the children you work with (i.e., puppets, flannelboard story, or stick puppets). Describe, carry out, and evaluate the activity using the following form.

Describe your literature experience.

_____

_____

_____

_____

Age group: _____

Objective: What will the children learn from this?

_____

_____

_____

_____

Procedures: How did you carry out this activity?

_____

_____

_____

_____

Evaluation: Did the activity turn out the way you planned? What changes would you make the next time you do this activity?

_____

_____

_____

_____

COMMUNICATION • Post-Training Wrap-Up

After completing this unit, review your personal goal and action plan from the beginning of the unit and describe how you accomplished your goal.

_____

_____

_____

_____

List at least three ways in which you changed your behavior as a result of your training in this Functional Area.

1. _____

2. _____

3. _____

COMMUNICATION • Professional Resource File

Resource Items

Collect the items for the Professional Resource File related to this Functional Area (if applicable). Refer to the pages at the back of this *Trainee's Manual* (pp. 281–283) and to the CDA booklet from the Council for Professional Recognition for specific instructions.

Statement of Competence

Write a short essay of 75 to 150 words, listing one or more goals you have for promoting children's communication abilities and describing activities you do to achieve these goals. Describe your experiences in your own words. Be concise. Use "I" statements—for example, "I read to children in small groups or individually every day. I have individual conversations with children throughout the day."

For additional information about writing your Statement of Competence, refer to the workbook section at the end of this *Trainee's Manual* (pp. 283–312) and to the CDA booklet from the Council for Professional Recognition.

Creative

Overview

Creativity means many things to many people. To some, it means artistic talent. To others, it means a passion to produce the original, discover joy, solve problems, appreciate beauty, seek out the unusual, or mold a product that is unique, beautiful, or inspiring.

Creativity and talent are not the same thing. *Talent* is the ability to perform easily and well in a particular area. *Creativity* is a more generalized trait that enables the individual to find new ways of arranging materials, asking questions, or solving problems. It is up to the teacher to structure an environment that nurtures and supports each child's innate creative spark.

Rationale

Whatever our definition, we all recognize that creativity is a highly desirable characteristic that we want to encourage in children. The child who is considered creative is treasured at home and in school. The bright child learns whatever we teach, but the highly creative child goes beyond our teaching and makes discoveries on her own.

This unit focuses on providing opportunities for children to exercise their creative abilities, to appreciate the creativity of others, and to explore and experiment with a variety of media, not only through art, music, and dramatic activities but in all aspects of the program. It demonstrates ways in which teachers can provide children with an array of experiences that stimulate their exploration and provide opportunities for children to express their creative ideas.

Objectives

- **Objective 1**   To use a variety of teaching techniques to encourage children to think and act creatively

- **Objective 2**   To recognize ways in which children from birth to age 5 express their creativity at each developmental stage and to identify caregiver behaviors and techniques that foster the development of creativity

- **Objective 3**   To describe materials and activities that encourage infants to explore and experiment

- **Objective 4**   To describe materials and activities that encourage toddlers to express their creativity

- **Objective 5**   To describe materials and activities that encourage preschool children to express their creativity

CREATIVE • Pretest

Answer each of the following True (T) or False (F).

_____ 1. There is no way to encourage creativity in infants.

_____ 2. A child who has no special talent is not creative.

_____ 3. One of the most effective ways to promote creativity at any age
is to encourage exploration.

_____ 4. Children who engage in pretend play are expressing their
creativity.

_____ 5. A good way to encourage creativity is to provide preschool
children with art, violin, and dance lessons.

_____ 6. Every child has the potential to be creative.

Place an "X" by each suggestion that promotes creativity.

_____ 1. Provide infants and toddlers with opportunities to play with
sensory materials.

_____ 2. Ask children open-ended questions.

_____ 3. Provide children with opportunities to experience beauty in art,
nature, and music.

_____ 4. Encourage children to find new ways of solving problems.

_____ 5. Encourage puppet play.

_____ 6. Provide children with opportunities to create original endings
to familiar stories.

Answer the following question.

What is the difference between *process* and *product* when providing children
with creative activities?

_____

_____

_____

CREATIVE • Self-Assessment

Indicate how you feel about your skills and abilities in each of the following categories by checking the appropriate column.

	Pretraining		
	Strong	**Satisfactory**	**Needs Improvement**
I can use a variety of teaching techniques to encourage children to think and act creatively.	☐	☐	☐
I recognize ways in which children from birth to age 5 express their creativity at each developmental stage and identify caregiver behaviors and techniques that foster the development of creativity.	☐	☐	☐
I can describe materials and activities that encourage infants to explore and experiment.	☐	☐	☐
I can describe materials and activities that encourage toddlers to express their creativity.	☐	☐	☐
I can describe materials and activities that encourage preschool children to express their creativity.	☐	☐	☐

CREATIVE • Pretraining Personal Goal

Based on your pretraining self-assessment, write a personal goal for this Functional Area and an action plan describing how you will accomplish the goal.

Goal _____

_____

_____

_____

Action Plan _____

_____

_____

_____

_____

_____

_____

_____

_____

_____

_____

_____

_____

Save your goal and action plan for the end of this unit so you will be able to answer these questions: How did you accomplish your goal? And how has your behavior changed based on your training?

To use a variety of teaching techniques to encourage children to think and act creatively

Jimmy's teacher was talking to the class about the need to be quiet during lunchtime. She explained to the class that the other teachers in the lunch-room had complained about their class being very loud talkers. She asked the class to suggest ways of solving the problem. "I know," said Jimmy, waving his hand. "We'll buy big bundles of cotton and stuff them in the teachers' ears."

Here are three ways Jimmy's teacher might have responded to his suggestion:

1. "Jimmy, don't be silly."
2. "Jimmy, please remember your manners."
3. "Jimmy, that is a clever idea, but I am not sure it would work. Teachers don't like cotton in their ears. Can you think of another idea?"

If her goal is to encourage creativity, which answer should Jimmy's teacher select? Why?

_____

_____

The teacher who encourages children to make suggestions and express their ideas has found an important way of encouraging creativity. Other teaching strategies that encourage creativity include the following:

1. Asking questions that have many possible answers
2. Giving children answers and encouraging them to think up questions to go with them
3. Showing children photos and asking them to decide what happened before each picture was taken and what will happen after

List three additional strategies to encourage creativity.

1. _____

2. _____

3. _____

Children demonstrate their creativity in many different ways. A creative teacher can even turn noncreative activities into activities that encourage creativity—for example:

Activity: Marching to music

Noncreative way: The teacher lines up all the children in a row. First, she shows them how to take marching steps in place. She puts on the music, and all the children march in place. Next, she shows them how to march single file. She turns on the music again, and the children march around the room single file.

Creative way: The children sit in a circle. The teacher says, "Let's pretend our hands are marching feet. Put your hands in front of you on the floor. Let's make our hands march to the music just like this. Very good. Who can think of another way to march to the music? With our elbows? That's a good idea—let's try it." The activity continues until the children have thought of several different ways of marching to the music (with their fingers, their wrists, their feet, while sitting, while standing, holding blocks or sticks and tapping on the floor).

It's your turn. Describe a creative way of doing each of these activities.

Activity: Each child makes a picture of a house.

Noncreative way: I am going to give you each a picture of a house. Color it in any way you want.

Creative way:

_____

_____

_____

_____

Activity: Teach children about what happens when you mail a letter.

Noncreative way: Talk to the children about how we put a letter in the mailbox and then the mail carrier comes with a truck, unlocks the mailbox, and empties it out.

Creative way:

_____

_____

_____

_____

Activity: Teach children how to make constructions out of blocks.

Noncreative way: "I like the way you children have been playing with the blocks and putting everything away neatly. Now I think the time has come to teach you something new and special that we can do with blocks. We are going to make a bridge. Now watch me. Does anyone in the room know how to make a bridge just like mine? Cassandra, do you know? Would you like to come up here and try? Very good. That's a fine bridge. Stuart, do you know? Would you like to come up here and try? Very good. That's a fine bridge. Who else would like a turn?"

Creative way:

_____

_____

_____

_____

As you filled in the blanks, struggling to think of a creative activity or the most creative way to accomplish a particular objective, you made an important discovery. You discovered that creativity can be thought about in two ways. We can think about encouraging creativity in children, and we can think about being creative in the way we teach children.

Here are some of the ways we can encourage creativity in children:

- Let children work with materials that can be molded or combined in a variety of ways.
- Encourage children to express their own ideas and find their own solutions.
- Show children one way of doing or making something and then challenge them to find different and more interesting ways.
- Ask children questions that have many different possible answers.
- Give children experiences that spark their curiosity and increase their sensitivity to the beauty and variety around them.

A second way we can be creative is to find creative ways of teaching children. We can be creative even when we are teaching children to solve a problem or answer a question with one correct answer. Let's look at a creative way of accomplishing a straightforward objective.

Objective: Help children learn to ask questions using the words *when, where, how,* and *why.*

Materials: An Ernie puppet and a toy telephone

Teacher (talking to a small group of children): "Ernie is on the telephone talking to Bert. Bert is asking him lots of questions."

Teacher (talking to the Ernie puppet): "Ernie, you are still talking to Bert?" (Teacher is making the Ernie puppet talk into a toy telephone)

Ernie (teacher talking for Ernie puppet in a high, squeaky voice): "Yes, I am; please don't interrupt me. Bert is asking me questions and I'm answering. Bert, my shoes are on my feet, where they always are. That's right, my shoes are on my feet."

Teacher (to class): "What question did Bert ask Ernie?"

Now it's your turn again. Here is an objective.

Objective: Children will demonstrate the meaning of each of the following prepositions—*in, out, over, under, behind, between.*

Creative way to teach the objective:

_____

_____

_____

_____

_____

_____

_____

Now you have the secret. The very best way to encourage creativity in the classroom is to discover and explore your own creative ideas.

To recognize ways in which children from birth to age 5 express their creativity at each developmental stage and to identify caregiver behaviors and techniques that foster the development of creativity

Creativity is often thought of only in terms of *products;* a creative child builds unique block structures, makes up original stories, or draws fanciful pictures. In actuality, creativity can also be thought of as a *process* or an *approach.* When parents, teachers, and other caregivers encourage exploration, promote self-expression, respect individual differences, value originality, and provide opportunities for experimentation, every child, from the moment of birth, has the potential of being creative.

A group of students enrolled in a community college were doing a unit on creativity. Their assignment was to observe five different classrooms and to write a short description of how each teacher encouraged creativity.

Annabelle and Horatio observed the same classrooms, but their descriptions of what they observed were very different:

Annabelle's List

Infant teacher: Played a Mozart tape.

Toddler teacher: Displayed the children's finger paintings on the wall.

Preschool teacher in Room A: Taught the children finger plays while they were waiting for lunch.

Preschool teacher in Room B: Made a really attractive bulletin board for the parents.

Horatio's List

Infant teacher: Gave two 10-month-old babies ice cubes to play with when they were sitting in their feeding tables.

Toddler teacher: Let the children choose the colors they wanted for their finger painting and played music while they painted.

Preschool teacher in Room A: While the children were waiting for their lunches to come from the cafeteria, she asked them to choose a finger play. After one round of "Eensy, Weensy Spider," she asked them how they could use their fingers to show how hard it was raining. When one of the boys started clapping, she asked him why he was clapping. When the boy explained that he was making a thunder clap, she told him that was a great idea. Then all the children started clapping and the lunch arrived.

Preschool teacher in Room B: The teacher put up two bulletin boards in the classroom: a small one for the parents and a large one in the pretend play area for the children. She explained to me that the children used the bulletin board with their pretend play themes. When they played "restaurant," they pinned up pictures of food to show their "customers" the specials for the day. When they played "doctor," they pinned up a diploma that came with the doctor's kit and a sign that said "Dokter iz in."

Look over these descriptions and identify two ways in which the students differed in their interpretation of creative teaching.

1. _____

_____

2. _____

_____

To describe materials and activities that encourage infants to explore and experiment

Infants, by nature, are curious, inventive, and resourceful. They love to try out new ways of doing things and new ways of making interesting things happen. They explore with their eyes, their hands, and their mouths and constantly try to discover how different things look, sound, feel, and taste. As we provide infants with interesting toys and materials and give them the opportunities to explore on their own, we are giving them opportunities to discover and express their own creativity.

List three ways in which infants explore their creativity.

1. The sounds they can make

_____

_____

2. The different things they can do with their hands

_____

_____

3. The different things that they can do with their bodies

_____

_____

Objective 4

To describe materials and activities that encourage toddlers to express their creativity

Mrs. Puzzled was complaining about the fact that when her toddler was given a present from one of her friends, he spent more time playing with the box than with the toy that was inside. Her friend had spent so much time looking for just the right toy, and she was so embarrassed!

Explain to Mrs. Puzzled what makes wrapping paper and boxes so attractive to toddlers.

_____

_____

_____

_____

_____

_____

A friend of Mrs. Give-Me was closing her nursery school. She asked Mrs. Give-Me if she would like to have some of the toys for her toddler group. "Oh, I'll be happy to take all the toys off your hands," Mrs. Give-Me answered promptly. Her friend explained, "I can't give you all of the toys because I have already promised several of my friends that I would give some to them. What I can do is show you a list of the toddler toys that I have in storage. You can pick whichever three you would like."

Help Mrs. Give-Me by identifying three toys on the following list that would be most likely to foster creativity. Also tell Mrs. Give-Me how the toys you have selected could encourage creativity.

A box of coloring books

A box of Barbie dolls

A set of unit blocks

A rocking horse

A big ride-on truck

A large basin that could be filled with water, sand, or cornmeal

A fish tank

A large collection of characters from Disney movies

A set of rhythm band instruments

A three-foot-tall teddy bear

1. _____

_____

2. _____

_____

3. _____

_____

To describe materials and activities that encourage preschool children to express their creativity

When we think about creativity in a preschool classroom, we are likely to think about the centers in the classroom devoted to art, music, construction, and imaginative play. While children can certainly express their creativity with the products they create, they are even more likely to express their creativity through the generation of new ideas, through the way they solve problems, through the unique ways they discover to use materials, and through their ability to view everyday occurrences from a unique perspective.

Miss Artsy was worried about Matilda. She couldn't carry a tune, she was hopeless when it came to art projects, she could never tell a story, and she was graceless when she tried to dance. Miss Artsy told her assistant teacher that Matilda was the least creative child she had ever known.

The assistant teacher decided to spend some time observing Matilda. Matilda had gone over to the dress-up corner and put on the bridal costume. Then she picked up a handkerchief from the dress-up trunk and placed it on her head like a veil. A minute later, she used the same handkerchief to put on pretend make-up and to shine her bridal slippers. Next she took off the wedding gown and went over to the housekeeping corner. "Gotta make a wedding cake," she muttered to no one in particular. "Gotta make a wedding cake." Matilda tucked the handkerchief into her jeans as an apron, took out an empty cake pan, pulled out the handkerchief, pretended to grease the pan, and then put the pan in the oven. As she waited for the cake to bake, she chanted a little ditty:

"Hurry up cake. You gotta bake. I am getting married today. Hurray!"

The assistant went back to Miss Artsy and told her about her observation. "You know," she said to the teacher, "I wouldn't call Matilda uncreative. She is one of the most creative children I have ever observed."

Who do you think is more accurate: Miss Artsy or the assistant? Explain your decision.

_____

_____

_____

_____

_____

_____

_____

CREATIVE • *Observation Opportunities*

Name _____

Observation Opportunity 1

Observe toddlers in water play. Describe at least five different ways in which they play with water.

1. _____

   _____

   _____

   _____

2. _____

   _____

   _____

   _____

3. _____

   _____

   _____

   _____

4. _____

   _____

   _____

   _____

5. _____

   _____

   _____

   _____

Observation Opportunity 2

Observe a child painting at an easel for a five-minute period. Complete the following sentences:

1. Used _____ different colors.

2. Described what she was doing with the following words:

   _____

   _____

   _____

   _____

   _____

3. Covered _____ portion of the paper with paint.

4. Used a _____ brush stroke.

5. The painting shows evidence of (representation elements, design, balance, etc.). Specify.

   _____

   _____

   _____

   _____

   _____

CREATIVE • Challenge Activities

Name _____

Challenge 1

Describe, carry out, and evaluate a music activity, a dramatic play activity, and a cooking activity in which children can show their creativity. Use the following worksheets to explain these activities.

Name of music activity: _____

Age group: _____

Description: What are you going to do?

_____

_____

Objective: What will the children learn from this?

_____

_____

Materials used:

_____

_____

Procedures: How did you carry out this activity?

_____

_____

_____

Evaluation: Did the activity turn out the way you planned? What changes would you make the next time you do this activity?

_____

_____

Name of dramatic play activity: _____

Age group: _____

Description: What are you going to do?

_____

_____

_____

_____

Objective: What will the children learn from this?

_____

_____

_____

Materials used:

_____

_____

_____

Procedures: How did you carry out this activity?

_____

_____

_____

_____

Evaluation: Did the activity turn out the way you planned? What changes would you make the next time you do this activity?

_____

_____

_____

_____

Name of cooking activity: _____

Age group: _____

Description: What are you going to do?

_____

_____

_____

_____

Objective: What will the children learn from this?

_____

_____

_____

Materials used:

_____

_____

_____

Procedures: How did you carry out this activity?

_____

_____

_____

_____

Evaluation: Did the activity turn out the way you planned? What changes would you make the next time you do this activity?

_____

_____

_____

_____

Challenge 2

Start your collection of play dough recipes by writing out two of your favorites.

Recipe 1

Name: _____

Ingredients: _____

_____

_____

_____

_____

Other materials needed: _____

_____

_____

Directions: _____

_____

_____

_____

_____

_____

Uses: _____

_____

_____

Recipe 2

Name: _____

Ingredients: _____

_____

_____

_____

_____

Other materials needed: _____

_____

_____

Directions: _____

_____

_____

_____

_____

_____

Uses: _____

_____

_____

CREATIVE • Post-Training Wrap-Up

After completing this unit, review your personal goal and action plan from the beginning of the unit and describe how you accomplished your goal.

_____

_____

_____

_____

List at least three ways in which you changed your behavior as a result of your training in this Functional Area.

1. _____

2. _____

3. _____

CREATIVE • Professional Resource File

Resource Items

Collect the items for the Professional Resource File related to this Functional Area (if applicable). Refer to the pages at the back of this *Trainee's Manual* (pp. 281–283) and to the CDA booklet from the Council for Professional Recognition for specific instructions.

Statement of Competence

Write a short essay of 75 to 150 words, listing one or more goals you have for promoting children's creativity and describing activities you do to achieve these goals. Describe your experiences in your own words. Be concise. Use "I" statements—for example, "I provide lots of dramatic play props so the children can be imaginative in their dress-up play. I give children lots of time with materials so they have enough time to be creative."

For additional information about writing your Statement of Competence, refer to the workbook section at the end of this *Trainee's Manual* (pp. 283–312) and to the CDA booklet from the Council for Professional Recognition.

The statements you have written for the chapters Physical, Cognitive, Communication, and Creative together make up the Competency Goal Statement for Goal II: To advance physical and intellectual competence.

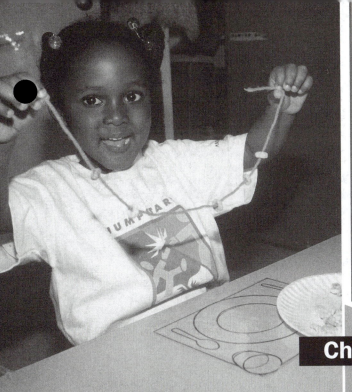

Chapter 8

Self

Overview

Self refers to the inner experiences, thoughts, feelings, sensations, and emotions that constitute each person's unique identity. *Self-concept* is an individual's mental image of his own characteristics and capabilities. *Self-esteem* refers to the child's self-evaluation.

Rationale

The feelings that a child develops about himself and about the people around him help to form his emotional makeup and have a direct bearing on his learning in school.

Infants vary in their inborn temperaments. Some are naturally easygoing and easy to soothe. Others are more sensitive, jittery, or feisty. Some quietly take in everything they see and hear; others seem to be always on the go. Some love novelty; others like predictability and are upset by too much change.

When parents and caregivers respond sensitively, babies learn to calm and rouse themselves appropriately and to experience the joy of mastering new skills. They come to love and trust those around them and to feel good about themselves. They learn eagerly and constantly. Babies whose cues are missed—who are ignored, overstimulated, or not given individual attention—fail to thrive. They may become depressed and withdrawn or constantly cranky and on edge. They may refuse to try new things or give up quickly, as if they expect to fail.

The self is thus a combination of inborn tendencies and life experiences. Parents, other family members, and early childhood teachers and caregivers all play critical roles in shaping whom a child will become.

Most children, regardless of family background, come to school with a sense of security and a rather well-defined concept of self. These are learned during their few, short years living with a family that is generally giving and supportive. It is the responsibility of the child care center and the individual teacher to provide experiences that continually affirm these positive feelings. Each child must feel love, security, acceptance, and respect from the adults with whom she interacts. The teacher helps each child to know, accept, and appreciate herself as an individual. The teacher helps each child develop a sense of awareness and self-esteem, to express and accept her own feelings—both good and bad—and to develop pride as an individual and as a member of a cultural or ethnic group.

The teacher interacts with each child many times during the course of a typical day in child care or school. It is critical that she be aware of the intimate relationship between self-concept and success in school and, indeed, success and competence in life. She must know that a child who feels incapable of success will not succeed and one who feels unworthy of affection or attention will not thrive. But the child who is made to feel special, who is loved and listened to and appreciated, will put forth her best efforts because she experiences joy in learning and pride in achievement.

Objectives

- **Objective 1** To recognize the sequence of emotional development from birth to 5 years and the role of the caregiver in supporting this development

- **Objective 2** To recognize ways in which infants develop trust and a sense of security

- **Objective 3** To recognize ways in which young toddlers develop self-awareness and learn to cope with separation

- **Objective 4** To recognize ways in which older toddlers develop a sense of autonomy

- **Objective 5** To recognize ways in which preschool children develop a sense of personal identity and self-worth, recognize and express their feelings, and take pride in their heritage

- **Objective 6** To recognize ways in which caregivers can help young children develop a sense of responsibility

- **Objective 7** To recognize ways in which teachers can create inclusive classrooms where all children are welcome

SELF • Pretest

Complete each of the following items as indicated.

1. Put an "X" before each statement that would have a positive effect on a child's self-concept. Star each statement that would have a negative effect.

_____ a. "Jimmy, I'm surprised at you. I thought you were too big to cry."

_____ b. "Now, Jimmy, you know you can tie your shoes. Your sister was the first one in the whole class last year to learn to tie her shoes."

_____ c. "I like the way you put your crayons away. Why don't you throw away the scrap of paper on your desk? Then your whole desk will be nice and clean."

_____ d. "You are the nicest child in the class."

_____ e. "You did a fine job playing the drums. You listened to the music and followed the beat very nicely."

_____ f. "Why did you throw that block across the classroom. Don't you have any sense?"

2. Put an "X" before each statement that is definitely true.

_____ a. Children should be toilet trained by 2 years.

_____ b. It is realistic to expect 4-year-olds to tie their own shoes.

_____ c. A 4-year-old child should ask an adult for help with dressing.

_____ d. Every child should achieve an appropriate balance between dependence and independence.

_____ e. A child who has not developed self-help skills appropriate for her age may be reacting either to a parent who expects too little or a parent who expects too much.

_____ f. Two-year-old boys who play with dolls probably have a poor self-image.

3. Describe three ways in which a caregiver can support an infant's emerging sense of self.

(1) _____

(2) _____

(3) _____

4. Here is a list of statements made by children. Use a star to show each child who is able to express feelings in an appropriate way.

_____ a. John: "I hate spinach. It's a yucky vegetable."

_____ b. Barbara: "He's mean. I'll bop him in the nose."

_____ c. John: "That movie made my tummy scared."

_____ d. Ethel: "That toy is mine because I played with it yesterday."

_____ e. Jean: "Mommy told me my cat got sick and I felt sad."

_____ f. Mary: "It's a pretty day outside. It makes me feel all dancy."

5. Match each activity on the left to the category on the right.

_____ (1) Activity that helps a child develop an accurate body image

_____ (2) Activity that helps a child learn to express bad feelings in a nonhurtful way

_____ (3) Activity that helps a child from another culture feel good about herself

_____ (4) Activity that helps a child who thinks of himself as awkward

A. Swaying to music, dramatic play, providing opportunities for the child to do well

B. Body parts puzzles, body prints, mirrors, photos, Simon Says games

C. Picture displays, books, learning languages from other cultures, playing music from a child's culture

D. Puppet play, "feeling wheel," modeling expression

SELF • Self-Assessment

Indicate how you feel about your skills and abilities in each of the following categories by checking the appropriate column.

	Pretraining		
	Strong	**Satisfactory**	**Needs Improvement**
I recognize the sequence of emotional development from birth to 5 years and the role of the caregiver in supporting this development.	☐	☐	☐
I recognize ways in which infants develop trust and a sense of security.	☐	☐	☐
I recognize ways in which young toddlers develop self-awareness and learn to cope with separation.	☐	☐	☐
I recognize ways in which older toddlers develop a sense of autonomy.	☐	☐	☐
I recognize ways in which preschool children develop a sense of personal identity and self-worth, recognize and express their feelings, and take pride in their heritage.	☐	☐	☐
I recognize ways in which caregivers can help young children develop a sense of responsibility.	☐	☐	☐
I recognize ways in which teachers can create inclusive classrooms where all children are welcome.	☐	☐	☐

SELF • Pretraining Personal Goal

Based on your pretraining self-assessment, write a personal goal for this Functional Area and an action plan describing how you will accomplish the goal.

Goal _____

_____

_____

_____

Action Plan _____

_____

_____

_____

_____

_____

_____

_____

_____

_____

_____

_____

Save your goal and action plan for the end of this unit so you will be able to answer these questions: How did you accomplish your goal? And how has your behavior changed based on your training?

Objective 1

To recognize the sequence of emotional development from birth to 5 years and the role of the caregiver in supporting this development

As in other developmental domains, the development of emotions follows a predictable sequence.

Using the Developmental Picture in your text, identify the approximate age for each of the emotional achievements listed.

a. Birth–8 months

b. 8–14 months

c. 14–24 months

d. 2–3 years

e. 3–5 years

_____ Discovers that she is an agent that can make things happen

_____ Learns to return a smile with a smile

_____ Takes the lead in initiating other people's reactions

_____ Shows emerging awareness of self by playing with his own hands or by touching his caregiver's mouth and then his own

_____ Is developing a sense of trust and learning to make predictions

_____ Responds to her mirror image by smiling and playing with the mirror

_____ Demonstrates a variety of emotions, including sadness, anger, surprise, and joy

_____ Recognizes herself in the mirror and wipes her own forehead if she sees a spot on it in the mirror

_____ Enjoys being praised and is upset when scolded

_____ Shows self-awareness by putting on a hat or a necklace

_____ Demonstrates shyness by hiding her head when a stranger talks to her

_____ Uses gestures, grunts, and some words to get an adult to respond to him

_____ Shows empathy when someone is hurt

_____ Uses words to express her feelings

_____ When he performs a stunt and people laugh, he performs the stunt again

_____ Uses the word _mine_ when someone picks up one of her toys

_____ Evaluates his own skills and compares himself to others

_____ Has temper tantrums when she can't have what she wants

_____ Is learning to make choices and say "no"

_____ Expresses a whole range of emotions: happy, worried, frightened, jealous, angry, sad, surprised

_____ Is able to express his feelings, needs, and desires

_____ Is able to make choices and control impulsive behaviors

_____ Tests limits by doing what she has been told not to do and watching the adult's reaction

_____ Asserts himself by insisting on doing things for himself or getting what he wants

Objective 2   To recognize ways in which infants develop trust and a sense of security

The development of trust begins at birth. As parents read their infants' cues and respond to their cries, infants come to recognize that their world is predictable and that they can make things happen.

Mrs. Pickerly had fed and diapered Jenna and put her in the crib. Although Jenna had closed her eyes during the feeding, she started to fuss when Mrs. Pickerly put her down for a nap. Mrs. Pickerly talked to her in a soft coo and patted her gently. Within seconds, Jenna was off to sleep.

As soon as Jenna was asleep, Pedro, age 8 months, awakened with a loud cry. Mrs. Pickerly went over to the crib. "You're okay, Pedro," Mrs. Pickerly said in a soothing voice as she lifted him out of the crib and held him on her shoulder. "Just what I thought, a big burp." Mrs. Pickerly put Pedro back in the crib and he fell asleep immediately.

Mrs. Pickerly sat on the chair beside the play area where Horatio, 13 months old, was playing with soft blocks. Horatio pulled himself up to a standing position and tossed a block over the gate. "No, no," Mrs. Pickerly said in a firm voice. "We do not throw blocks." Horatio pointed to the block and looked expectantly at Mrs. Pickerly. "No way am I going to pick that up for you, " Mrs. Pickerly said crossly. "If you wanted to play with it, you shouldn't have thrown it down."

Describe one way in which Mrs. Pickerly acted appropriately and one way in which she acted inappropriately.

Appropriately: _____

_____

Inappropriately: _____

_____

Objective 3

To describe ways in which young toddlers develop self-awareness and learn to cope with separation

Before a child can really feel good about himself, he must have a sense of being an individual person who has an identity and of being an agent who has the power to make things happen. The development of a sense of identity begins with body awareness. What do I look like? How am I similar and how am I different from other people? What do other people see when they look at me? What are the parts of my body, and how do they fit together?

Complete each of the following by describing an activity that helps develop a positive body image.

1. A mirror game

   _____

2. An activity song

   _____

3. An exercise

   _____

4. A series of photos

   _____

5. A craft that involves tracing or making a print of some part of your body

   _____

Being dropped off at child care and watching her parent leave the room may be particularly traumatic for a toddler. This is especially true when the toddler is brought to child care for the first time or when a toddler who has been accustomed to child care and developed a good relationship with one or more of the caregivers discovers that her special caregiver is no longer there. While some children may be able to make a quick adjustment to separation, others will find it quite traumatic.

For each incident described below, suggest a practical way of making separation easier for the toddler and the parent.

Situation 1: Theodore has just turned 2, and in accordance with the usual procedure at the Follow-the-Rules Child Care Center, he is being moved to the "big boy" room. When he walks into the room with his mother and sees children and caregivers he doesn't know, he throws himself on the floor and has a full-fledged tantrum.

_____

_____

Situation 2: Mrs. Darling brought her 14-month-old daughter, Katrina, to the Family Child Care Home. As usual, Katrina got teary when her mother said good-bye. Mrs. Darling picked her up immediately and told her that she would be back very soon. The family care provider brought over a teddy bear that Katrina loved to play with and suggested that the teddy bear was hungry and they had better go and make him some breakfast. Katrina stopped crying and started to talk to the teddy bear. Mrs. Darling told the caregiver that Katrina had a little sniffle and probably shouldn't go outside during the day. She picked up Katrina again and said, "I will give you one last hug, and then I have to go." Katrina started crying again and clung to her mother.

_____

_____

Situation 3: Darren was 20 months old and was used to going to child care. He ran to the caregiver and gave her a big hug and started walking to the block area and joined some boys who were building a castle. His father said, "Good-bye, Darren. I will see you later." Darren played happily with the children for the rest of the day. When Darren's father came to pick him up in the afternoon, Darren started to cry. "Go away, Daddy. I stay." His father was upset. He pulled Darren by the arm and dragged him out of the center.

_____

_____

To recognize ways in which older toddlers develop a sense of autonomy

At 2 years old, children are recognizing that they can make choices, manage some things without adult help, and make other people do their bidding. While some people talk about this need for autonomy as "terrible two's" behavior, students of child development recognize that this "no" stage or this "I can do it myself" stage is an indicator of healthy development. When a 2-year-old says "no," he is demonstrating his emerging ability to make choices and arrive at decisions. When a 2-year-old says "I do it myself," she is demonstrating a desire to do things on her own and develop her own competence.

Mrs. Frazzled arrived at the child care center with her 2-year-old 20 minutes late on a field trip day. "I'm really sorry to be late," she told the teacher, "but Theresa is going through a terrible stage. The first thing that happened this morning was that Theresa took forever getting dressed. She insisted upon putting on her own socks and she had trouble getting her heels in. Then we went to breakfast and she pushed away the orange juice, saying 'No, apple juice.' When I gave her the apple juice, she wanted the orange juice. Then, when her cousin Pedro, who had lost his lunch box, put his lunch in her lunch box, she shouted 'mine,' pulled it away from him, and had a tantrum. I gave the lunch box back to Pedro and explained to Theresa that she gets a hot lunch at school and doesn't need a lunch box. It did no good. She kept on screaming and kicking, and I had to carry her into the car. She used to be such a sweet child and now she's a monster. Should I bring her to a psychiatrist?"

In a few words, help Mrs. Frazzle recognize that Theresa's behavior is just what you would expect from a 2-year-old.

_____

_____

Suggest two effective ways of managing Theresa when she says "no" or "mine."

1. _____

2. _____

Now suggest two ways of managing Theresa when she insists of doing things by herself.

1. _____

2. _____

Toddlers and preschoolers experience strong feelings as they grow and may swing rapidly from one extreme to the other: independence/dependence, hostility/love, anger/tenderness, aggression/passivity. Young children need to have secure relationships with parents and caregivers to help them cope with these intense emotions. Adults can help by staying calm through a child's emotional reactions, by supplying words that a child can use to express her feelings, and by reading or telling stories about other children's emotional experiences.

A major difference between adults and children is that adults have had more experience with feelings and are more accurate than children in identifying their own feelings. A child who is angry may break something or push a child down without recognizing that what he is experiencing is a feeling of anger. On the other hand, a child may be bouncing all over the room and failing to get involved in a task without realizing that he is feeling a sense of joy and exhilaration. As children learn to identify their own feelings and to accept them as legitimate, they also learn ways of expressing their feelings in positive ways.

Describe how the following materials or situations can be used to help a child learn to recognize different feelings or emotions.

1. A "feeling wheel," which can be dialed to point to a serious face, an angry face, or a happy face

   _____

   _____

   _____

2. A children's storybook

   _____

   _____

   _____

3. A quiet chat with a child

   _____

   _____

   _____

To recognize ways in which preschool children develop a sense of personal identity and self-worth, recognize and express their feelings, and take pride in their heritage

It is important for teachers to help children learn to recognize their own individuality. It is even more important for teachers to help children feel good about themselves and about their families. Feeling good about yourself or having a positive self-image is the outcome of life experiences. People with a positive self-image believe in their own adequacy and feel positive about their future. Parents and teachers have a powerful influence on the way young children feel about themselves.

Mrs. Walters walked into the preschool with Karen in her arms. Mrs. Whitefield, the teacher of the 4-year-olds, was waiting at the door.

Both Mrs. Walters and Mrs. Whitefield are concerned about Karen being happy on her first day of school. Unfortunately, some of Mrs. Walter's behavior may be tearing down, rather than building up, Karen's self-image.

Be a sleuth. Go over the transcript below and underline things that Mrs. Walters says or does that could be damaging Karen's self-image.

Mrs. Whitefield: "Hello. You must be Mrs. Walters. And this must be Karen. I am so happy that you are joining our class, Karen. We have a very good time in here."

Mrs. Walters: "You know, Karen is really a shy child, and it takes her quite a while to warm up to strangers. Karen, turn your head around like my sweet pumpkin and say hello to your new teacher." (Karen buries her head in her mother's blouse.)

Mrs. Whitefield: "Karen, we have a bunny in our classroom named Cotton Puff. Why don't you and your mommy come and look at Cotton Puff. I think she would like some breakfast."

Mrs. Walters: "Karen is a little nervous around animals. Why don't I just stay here this morning to help her get adjusted. You know this kind of experience can be frightening for a shy child like Karen. Once children have trouble with the first day of school, they build up a fear of school that can last a lifetime. That happened to Karen's brother, Jeremiah. He spent the whole first day at nursery school crying, and he's hated school ever since."

Mrs. Whitefield: "I am happy you can stay with Karen for a while. I know you will help Karen find things she likes to play with. Oh look, Karen.

I found a puzzle with fruit on it. I bet you can put this puzzle together all by yourself. (Mrs. Whitefield holds out her arms and Karen goes to her. Mrs. Whitefield places Karen at a small table and gives her a three-piece puzzle. Karen completes it in a few seconds.) I was right. You are a fine puzzle putter-togetherer. I better find a harder puzzle."

Mrs. Walters: "There, Karen, I told you school isn't as bad as you thought. Oh, some other children are coming in now. Okay, Karen, stay close to Mommy. I won't let those big kids bother you."

Read the following list of remarks made by caregivers to children in a child care center. Put a star by each remark that would have a positive effect on a child's self-image.

_____ "I like the way you began this drawing. I would love to see it again when you've drawn a little more."

_____ "Good job. You put almost all the blocks away. Would you like me to help you finish?"

_____ "Your job was to put the blocks away. How come you didn't finish?"

_____ "Not again! This is the third time you've started a drawing that you haven't finished. You are so wasteful! If you don't plan to finish, you shouldn't begin."

_____ "Don't tell me it's going to be one of those days. Did you get enough sleep last night?"

_____ "You are feeling tired. Would you like to sit down for a few minutes and read a book?"

_____ "You worked hard on that puzzle. You put four pieces in all by yourself. If you would like, I can help you finish it."

_____ "Don't get so upset about not being able to pump the swing. You are good at coloring."

_____ "You are upset because you can't pump the swing. This time, when I give you a push, try straightening your legs and leaning back. You'll get the knack pretty soon."

_____ "You wet your pants *again?* When are you going to grow up?"

No matter how much children enjoy being in child care, very few of them love it more than being home. Likewise, few children value the affection of their caregivers more than they value the affection of their own parents. Home for children is their base of security. It is the place that makes them feel most important and most worthy. When a caregiver implies in any way that there is something wrong with a child's home or family, the child may be devastated. In order to make children feel that you value their homes and families, you need to find positive ways of getting to know about their home lives.

It isn't enough to simply avoid saying negative things. The caregiver who says "If I don't like a child's family, I just don't talk about it" may be putting the child down. One way of making children feel good about their homes and their families is to provide opportunities for culture sharing. Give children opportunities to talk about their families or to invite family members to school. Make sure that there are pictures, photos, artifacts, and books in your classroom that reflect the children's cultures. Invite parents and children to bring items from home to share with the class that reflect family histories and traditions.

A second way to make children feel good about their homes and their families is to demonstrate your appreciation of diversity. Often, this involves answering difficult questions and handling sensitive issues.

*How could you respond to each of these questions in a respectful way?**

1. "Why does Jamie wear those funny things in her ears?" (The child is pointing at Jamie's hearing aids.)

   _____

   _____

2. "Why does José talk funny?"

   _____

   _____

3. "Jesse says that you aren't supposed to celebrate Christmas. Is she right?"

   _____

   _____

4. "Why is Alicia's skin brown?"

   _____

   _____

*Refer to brochure #565 from NAEYC: Derman-Sparks, L., Gutierrez, M., & Brunson Day, C. (reprint 2001). *Teaching Young Children to Resist Bias.*

Competency Goal III • To support social and emotional development and provide positive guidance

5. "How come Jimmy is playing with a doll? Dolls are girl toys."

_____

_____

Objective 6

To recognize ways in which caregivers can help young children develop a sense of responsibility

We need to know the approximate age when children develop different self-help skills and identify children who need to work on these skills. The appropriate age for achieving self-help skills is influenced by geography and community. Begin your self-help program by solidifying your own beliefs about when children should acquire different self-help skills.

Before each statement, write the appropriate age for achievement.

_____ Out of diapers during the day

_____ Completely toilet trained, day and night

_____ Completely off bottle or breast

_____ Bathes herself with supervision

_____ Bathes himself without supervision

_____ Crosses a quiet road alone

_____ Crosses a major intersection alone

_____ Feeds herself

_____ Dresses himself, except for shoes

_____ Dresses herself, including shoes

_____ Brushes his teeth without supervision

_____ Washes his own hair without supervision

_____ Plays outside near the house by herself

_____ Goes to the corner store by himself

_____ Fills the bathtub with water

_____ Stays alone in the house

_____ Opens up the refrigerator and takes something out

_____ Makes her own breakfast

_____ Makes his own lunch

To recognize ways in which teachers can create inclusive classrooms where all children are welcome

Creating an *inclusive classroom* starts with focusing on meeting each child's unique developmental needs and building on each child's individual strengths and interests. These are both goals that all child care professionals should work toward.

Accommodating children with special needs doesn't pose a problem in such an individualized atmosphere. But challenges may arise in trying to reach our goals when serving these children.

For each of the following scenarios, help the teacher figure out what to do to address the challenge that's been presented.

Ms. Singer has been trying hard to get one of her students, 3-year-old Alex, who has a vision impairment, to participate in circle time activities. He seems to enjoy being in the group and singing the songs. But whenever Ms. Singer calls on him—for instance, to ask what song he wants to sing—he won't say a word.

_____

_____

_____

_____

_____

Four-year-old Jeanine has cerebral palsy and uses a walker and sometimes crutches, as well. Her mother, Mrs. Let-Go, wants Jeanine's teacher to make her join in active play outdoors. Right now, Jeanine just stays in one place and won't be coaxed into participating in outdoor activities.

_____

_____

_____

_____

_____

SELF • Observation Opportunities

Name _____

Observation Opportunity 1

Observe an infant with a caregiver. Complete the following checklist.

	Yes	No	Describe what you saw that brought you to this conclusion.
The infant engages in back-and-forth conversation.	☐	☐	_____ _____
The infant responds positively to a consistent caregiver.	☐	☐	_____ _____
The infant is able to make his wants known to a caregiver.	☐	☐	_____ _____
The infant when crying quiets when he sees or hears his caregiver.	☐	☐	_____ _____
The infant initiates back-and-forth conversation.	☐	☐	_____ _____

Observation Opportunity 2

Observe a child for 30 minutes. Record anything that the child does or says that reflects his self-image. Star each observation that you feel could indicate a positive self-concept.

Age of child: _____

Observations:

_____

_____

_____

_____

_____

_____

_____

_____

_____

_____

_____

_____

_____

_____

_____

_____

_____

_____

_____

_____

_____

SELF • Challenge Activities

Name _____

Challenge 1

Identify (or develop), try out, and evaluate an activity, educational material, or toy (other than a book) that promotes positive feelings or helps children cope with difficulties. Complete the following worksheet.

Name of activity, educational material, or toy: _____

Age group: _____

Description of item: _____

_____

_____

_____

Objective: What will the children learn from this? How can this item be used to promote positive feelings or help children cope with difficulties?

_____

_____

_____

Procedures: How will this item be presented to the children?

_____

_____

_____

Evaluation: Did the activity turn out the way you planned? What changes would you make the next time you do this activity?

_____

_____

_____

Challenge 2

Find a book that helps a child with a situation that might be upsetting, such as divorce, a death in the family, a new baby, or going to the hospital. Complete the following worksheet to describe your book.

Title of book: _____

Author: _____

Illustrator: _____

Publisher's name: _____   **Date published:** _____

Age group that would enjoy this book: _____

Type of book: _____

How does the book check out for antibias themes?

_____

_____

What is the book about? How will this book help a child who is going through a difficult situation?

_____

_____

_____

_____

_____

_____

_____

_____

● **SELF** • **Post-Training Wrap-Up**

After completing this unit, review your personal goal and action plan and describe how you accomplished your goal.

_____

_____

_____

_____

List at least three ways in which you changed your behavior as a result of your training in this Functional Area.

1. _____

2. _____

3. _____

● **SELF** • **Professional Resource File**

Resource Items

Collect the items for the Professional Resource File related to this Functional Area (if applicable). Refer to the pages at the back of this *Trainee's Manual* (pp. 281–283) and to the CDA booklet from the Council for Professional Recognition for specific instructions.

Statement of Competence

Write a short essay of 75 to 150 words, listing one or more goals you have for yourself and for children and families in the area of Self and describing activities you do to achieve these goals. Describe your experiences in your own words. Be concise. Use "I" statements—for example, "I try to help each child feel special. I always greet and hug children as they arrive and help them get involved in play."

For additional information about writing your Statement of Competence, refer to the workbook section at the end of this *Trainee's Manual* (pp. 283–312) and to the CDA booklet from the Council for Professional Recognition.

Chapter 9

Social

Overview

Social development refers to the growth of the child's ability to make and maintain friends and to develop mutually supportive relationships with adults and children. It also includes learning to work and play cooperatively with children and adults and to assume the role of either leader or follower.

Rationale

Preschool children are *egocentric*—that is, they see the world from their own point of view and have difficulty understanding a point of view that is different from their own. A typical example of this is the 3-year-old who holds a painting up to the phone and asks her Nana to admire it.

Because children are unable to recognize the point of view of someone else does not mean, however, that they are unable to be kind, cooperative, and empathetic. Children are natural mimics and talented actors. They can imitate the behavior of a kind and nurturant model and play the role of another person. The adult who is concerned with the development of social skills in young children must serve as a positive model and at the same time structure an environment in which children have the opportunity to learn how other people act and feel.

Objectives

- **Objective 1**   To recognize the sequence of social skill development from birth to 5 years and the role of the caregiver in supporting this development

- **Objective 2**   To recognize ways in which infants and toddlers develop meaningful relationships with parents, caregivers, and other children

- **Objective 3**   To recognize ways of encouraging preschool children to make friends and engage in social play

- **Objective 4**   To help children build on their strengths and overcome their difficulties

- **Objective 5**   To describe ways in which caregivers can encourage helping, sharing, and caring behaviors among children

- **Objective 6**   To design a classroom environment and curriculum that support cooperative behavior

SOCIAL • Pretest

Answer each of the following True (T) or False (F).

_____ 1. It is good to have young children in large groups for most activities.

_____ 2. A primary way to teach young children about social skills is to model social skills.

_____ 3. It is best *not* to plan social activities; they just happen.

_____ 4. Toddlers should learn to share if they are in a child care setting.

_____ 5. You should place children together if you notice a friendship emerging.

Select the best answer for each of the following.

_____ 1. In order to teach children how to play together, a teacher should:
  a. make children say "I'm sorry" if they hurt another child.
  b. not allow friends to play together.
  c. provide large chunks of time for children to play.
  d. have a teacher-directed activity where the children are told how to treat their friends.

_____ 2. Which toy/material best encourages children to play together?
  a. Dramatic play equipment
  b. Coloring books
  c. A pegboard
  d. A wind-up toy

Match each environment on the left to the appropriate play type on the right.

_____ 1. A shelf of manipulative materials   A. large group

_____ 2. A cozy area with a big pillow   B. individual or small group

_____ 3. Easels in the art area   C. small group

_____ 4. A well-defined space for dance and   D. individual
         movement

_____ 5. A construction area with blocks

SOCIAL • Self-Assessment

Indicate how you feel about your skills and abilities in each of the following categories by checking the appropriate column.

	Pretraining		
	Strong	**Satisfactory**	**Needs Improvement**
I recognize the sequence of social skill development from birth to 5 years and the role of the caregiver in supporting this development.	☐	☐	☐
I recognize ways in which infants and toddlers develop meaningful relationships with parents, caregivers, and other children.	☐	☐	☐
I recognize ways of encouraging preschoolers to make friends and engage in social play.	☐	☐	☐
I can help children build on their strengths and overcome their difficulties.	☐	☐	☐
I can describe ways in which caregivers can encourage helping, sharing, and caring behaviors among children.	☐	☐	☐
I can design a classroom environment and curriculum that support cooperative behavior.	☐	☐	☐

SOCIAL • Pretraining Personal Goal

Based on your pretraining self-assessment, write a personal goal for this Functional Area and an action plan describing how you will accomplish the goal.

Goal _____

_____

_____

_____

Action Plan _____

_____

_____

_____

_____

_____

_____

_____

_____

_____

_____

_____

Save your goal and action plan for the end of this unit so you will be able to answer these questions: How did you accomplish your goal? And how has your behavior changed based on your training?

To recognize the sequence of social skill development from birth to 5 years and the role of the caregiver in supporting this development

The responsive relationship that develops when a caregiver plays with a baby provides the foundation for the child's enjoyment of social interaction. From infancy on, children pay special attention to what their peers are doing. Babies enjoy watching other babies and are likely to save their biggest smile for a playful sibling. Although babies cannot talk to their peers and share their play ideas, caregivers of children suggest that babies as young as 10 months old may select favorite peers.

Toddlers between 1 and 2 years old often enjoy playing with other children. Although they are too young to understand about taking turns and sharing toys, they love to romp together and imitate each other. A favorite activity for toddlers may be pulling the toys off the shelf or emptying a basket of blocks.

Between 2 and 3 years old, we are likely to see children engage in *parallel play*. This is where children play with the same kinds of toys and keep careful watch of each other. Although children who engage in parallel play may not be ready to share their toys, they are ready to share the fun of playing together.

Mrs. Better-Safe-Than-Sorry was looking through toy catalogs. She had received a donation of money from the church and was trying to decide whether to buy several of the same toys for each classroom, so that the children wouldn't fight, or to buy several different toys for each classroom, so that the children would learn to share.

Help Mrs. Better-Safe-Than-Sorry select the right toys. For each age level, indicate the choice of toys that is most likely to encourage interaction.

Infants

_____ Choice 1: Two each of the same balls, "busy boards," and stacking toys

_____ Choice 2: Eight different baby toys, including one rattle, one mirror, one "busy board," one telephone, one ball, one stacking toy, one drum, and one squeeze toy

Young toddlers (14–24 months)

_____ Choice 1: One large wagon and one set of large cardboard blocks

_____ Choice 2: One pegboard, one inset puzzle, one pull toy, one telephone, and one small piano

Older toddlers (2-year-olds)

_____ Choice 1: One sandbox with three shovels, three pails, and three funnels

_____ Choice 2: One tricycle and one swing

3- and 4-year-olds

_____ Choice 1: One large set of wooden unit blocks

_____ Choice 2: A large tray of individual puzzles

Objective 2

To recognize ways in which infants and toddlers develop meaningful relationships with parents, caregivers, and other children

Mrs. Butterfly brought her toddler to a family child care home for the first time. She was surprised that the only other children in the home were an 8-month-old infant, a 4-year-old girl, and a 5-year-old boy. The caregiver talked to her son for a few minutes and then asked Mrs. Butterfly if she had any concerns. "The only thing that bothers me," she told the caregiver, "is that there are no other toddlers for Darien to play with."

Please help the caregiver allay Mrs. Butterfly's fears.

_____

_____

_____

_____

_____

Fortunately, by the time the caregiver explained that Darien would be fine, the 4-year-old had taken Darien by the hand and walked him over to the toy shelf.

To recognize ways of encouraging preschool children to make friends and engage in social play

Mrs. Green was having problems. One of her parents, Mrs. Snoozledoff, had complained to the director. She found Mrs. Green's class to be very disorganized. "Every time I go in there," she complained, "I see children working by themselves or in small groups. Everybody is doing something different. Instead of standing up there and teaching the class something, like a good teacher would, that Mrs. Green just stands around puttering with materials or talking to the kids. Those kids like it in the classroom, but boy will they be in trouble when they get to real school."

Help Mrs. Green. What can she say to the director to justify her organization of the classroom?

_____

_____

You are right! Mrs. Green has nothing to apologize for. Children need the opportunities she provides to work individually and in small groups.

Working in Groups

When you think about children working in groups, do you visualize a situation in which they are at tables or sitting around in a circle and the teacher is directing the activity? This is one way but not the only way of encouraging children to work together in groups. Another way of doing so is to structure the environment and set up activities that encourage a few children to work together on a project or play together in an activity area.

Describe one more effective way of encouraging 3- and 4-year-old children to play cooperatively.

_____

_____

Working Individually

Encouraging individual play can be even more difficult than encouraging group cooperation. Sometimes, young children have difficulty functioning independently. Problems can arise when children require too much attention from an adult, when they interfere with each other's work, or when they begin something that they can't finish.

Individual work is best under these conditions:

1. A way is provided for children to mark off their own workspaces; small tables, trays, or individual mats can be used.
2. The shelves and materials are coded so that children find it easy to put things back on the shelves in the right way.
3. A plan is worked out to help children select work that is not too difficult for them to complete.

Describe one more effective way of encouraging individual play.

_____

_____

To help children build on their strengths and overcome their difficulties

Mrs. Stiffcollar was in charge of the parents' meeting at the We-Care Center. Following the meeting, several mothers from the 4-year-old classroom began asking questions about their children.

Please help Mrs. Stiffcollar answer their questions. She knows a lot about infants, but she isn't too familiar with 4-year-olds.

"My Bartholomew seems to me to be a born leader. He is always full of good ideas, and the children in the neighborhood always want to play with him. My problem is my neighbor. She says that I shouldn't let my son be so bossy. I should teach him to listen to the other children and follow their ideas. Is the neighbor right?"

_____

_____

"My problem is different. Anthony has always been a quiet and timid child. He and his friend Terry spend hours together, building with Legos or pretending they are zoo keepers. In school, he's the same way. He finds one other boy to play with, and they go off together and never play in a large group. Should I try to find a counselor for him?"

_____

_____

"My kid is a loner, just like his father. He likes to do things his own way, and he doesn't want any other kids around messing up his things. There's nothing wrong with that, is there?"

_____

_____

Pretending is the natural language of preschool children. It provides them with a way of having fun, of learning about their world, of coping with problems and concerns, and of making lasting friends. It is through pretending that children learn to take a different point of view and to make distinctions between what is real and what is fantasy.

Pretending is most likely to flourish in a classroom when the following conditions exist (complete each phrase):

The teacher enjoys _____

_____

The teacher provides experiences that spark pretending, like _____

_____

and _____

_____

The teacher identifies and collects props that _____

_____

The teacher provides the space _____

_____

To describe ways in which caregivers can encourage helping, sharing, and caring behaviors among children

While many child caregivers, as well as parents, are concerned with academic ability, new research on competency in early childhood supports the position that social and emotional development are the foundation of all later learning. One of the qualities that we associate with *social competence* is the ability to express our own feelings and appreciate the feelings of others.

It is sometimes difficult for children to recognize and differentiate their own feelings. A child who becomes aggressive may not recognize that he is feeling frustrated and inadequate. A child who is exuberant may not recognize that she is seeking an outlet for her happy feelings.

Here are some suggestions for helping children recognize and describe their feelings:

1. Talk about an event that happened with an individual child. Reflect on the feelings the child may have experienced.
2. Read a story and ask the children how each of the characters feels when something good or bad happens.
3. Play a record and ask the children to tell you when the music is happy or sad.
4. Ask the children to make pictures with colors that make them feel sad. Ask the children to make pictures with colors that make them happy.
5. Provide opportunities in your classroom for dress-up, role-playing, and puppet play.
   a. Dress-up corners provide children with opportunities to try out different roles. By pretending to be a mother, daddy, firefighter, police officer, and so on, children are given opportunities to try out other roles.
   b. Role-playing is like dress-up, only the activity is usually more structured. For role-play to work with preschool children, the teacher must be part of the action.
   c. Children can learn about emotions by using puppets that have television or movie personalities (Oscar the Grouch and Eeyore the Miserable Donkey). Homemade puppets can also be used, and the children can develop skills in using them to express their feelings.

List three other ways to help children describe their feelings.

1. _____
2. _____
3. _____

To design a classroom environment and curriculum that support cooperative behavior

Whether a teacher is planning for a group of young toddlers, older toddlers, or preschool-aged children, the way she sets up the environment and implements the curriculum has a major influence on how well the children will learn to cooperate with each other.

Select an age range between 1 and 5 years old, and describe three ways in which the teacher can support cooperation.

Age group: _____

1. _____

2. _____

3. _____

SOCIAL • Observation Opportunity

Name _____

Observe a toddler or a preschool child with one or more other children. Then complete the following sentences.

The child initiated interaction with another child by:

_____

_____

_____

_____

The child responded to the play overtures of another child by:

_____

_____

_____

_____

The child maintained interactions by:

_____

_____

_____

_____

The child broke off interactions by:

_____

_____

_____

_____

SOCIAL • Challenge Activities

Name _____

Challenge 1

List five activities or play materials that promote social interaction for your age group, and give your rationale for each selection.

1. _____

   Rationale: _____

   _____

   _____

2. _____

   Rationale: _____

   _____

   _____

3. _____

   Rationale: _____

   _____

   _____

4. _____

   Rationale: _____

   _____

   _____

5. _____

   Rationale: _____

   _____

   _____

Challenge 2

Write out your basic schedule/routine. Describe the opportunities provided for social interaction during each of these major blocks of time.

Time	Activity	Opportunity for social interaction

SOCIAL • Post-Training Wrap-Up

After completing this unit, review your personal goal and action plan and describe how you accomplished your goal.

_____

_____

_____

_____

List at least three ways in which you changed your behavior as a result of your training in this Functional Area.

1. _____

2. _____

3. _____

SOCIAL • Professional Resource File

Resource Items

Collect the items for the Professional Resource File related to this Functional Area (if applicable). Refer to the pages at the back of this *Trainee's Manual* (pp. 281–283) and to the CDA booklet from the Council for Professional Recognition for specific instructions.

Statement of Competence

Write a short essay of 75 to 150 words, listing one or more goals you have for yourself and for the children and families in social development and describing activities you do to achieve these goals. Describe your experiences in your own words. Be concise. Use "I" statements—for example, "I set up informal situations that encourage children to cooperate, such as asking two to three children to work together to set up the table for snack. I set the tone for clean-up time as an opportunity for children to help one another, rather than insisting that each child clean up only his or her playthings."

For additional information about writing your Statement of Competence, refer to the workbook section at the end of this *Trainee's Manual* (pp. 283–312) and to the CDA booklet from the Council for Professional Recognition.

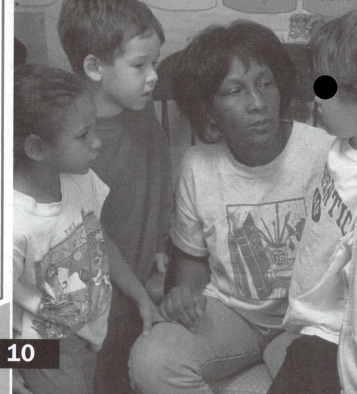

Competency Goal III
To support social and emotional development and provide positive guidance

Chapter 10

Guidance

Overview

Guidance involves helping children learn and practice appropriate behaviors that contribute to their own well-being and the well-being of others.

Rationale

One of the major challenges that teachers face is to create and maintain a climate within their child care setting where children are happy and productive and where stress and confrontation are limited. Teachers seek to achieve this goal in many different ways, depending on the ages and characteristics of the children and the number of children they are responsible for. Infant caregivers recognize the importance of creating an environment that is basically quiet and soothing. Toddler caregivers recognize the importance of arranging and equipping the classroom to invite cooperative play and minimize disputes over toys. Preschool teachers find it helpful to develop classroom rules that emphasize responsibility and define acceptable behaviors.

A second challenge that all teachers face is identifying ways of redirecting behavior that is negative or nonproductive. Again, the techniques that teachers use depend on the ages and characteristics of the children. The one rule of thumb for all child caregivers, however, is that the guidance techniques we use must be positive. The goal of guidance is not to punish bad behavior but to help children learn ways of achieving their own goals while respecting the rights of others.

New research has shown that *emotional intelligence* is the most important predictor of school readiness and of life success. Emotional intelligence involves the ability to handle stress without falling apart, to know right from wrong, to control impulses and exert self-discipline, to keep working in the face of challenge, to recognize one's own feelings and those of others, and to empathize with and take care of others. These abilities begin to take shape in the first year of life. Teachers and caregivers of infants, toddlers, and preschoolers play a critical role in guiding their development.

Objectives

- **Objective 1**   To identify ways of helping infants achieve self-regulation and develop coping skills

- **Objective 2**   To identify ways of helping young toddlers explore their world and make new discoveries without being destructive or wasteful and without causing injury to themselves or others

- **Objective 3**   To help older toddlers cope with fear, anger, and frustration and strike a balance between their longing for nurturance and desire to be independent

- **Objective 4**   To learn ways of helping preschool children recognize and value differences, resolve conflicts, express their feelings in words, and accept reasonable limits

- **Objective 5**   To recognize ways of using positive guidance techniques to reduce children's unwanted behaviors

- **Objective 6**   To recognize ways of providing positive guidance for children whose families use styles of discipline that are different from those the teacher has been taught

GUIDANCE • Pretest

Complete each of the following items as indicated.

1. Describe one important concept to consider in setting up guidelines for a preschool classroom.

   _____

   _____

2. Describe two things you can do in your classroom that will encourage self-discipline in your children.

   a. _____

   b. _____

3. Describe two positive guidance techniques for guiding children's behavior.

   a. _____

   b. _____

4. How can a teacher help children use words to express their wants and needs?

   _____

   _____

5. Put an "X" by each statement that describes a good way of helping infants with stranger or separation anxiety.

   _____ a. Make sure that the infant has opportunities to be taken care of by several caregivers.

   _____ b. When a parent leaves and the child rejects your efforts to comfort him, it is best to just leave him alone.

   _____ c. Explain to the parent the importance of talking to you in a confident way and saying good-bye cheerfully to the infant.

   _____ d. When an infant is upset because her parent has left, hold her lovingly and let her cry for a while before getting her interested in a new toy.

   _____ e. Play Peek-a-Boo frequently.

GUIDANCE • Self-Assessment

Indicate how you feel about your skills and abilities in each of the following categories by checking the appropriate column.

	Pretraining		
	Strong	**Satisfactory**	**Needs Improvement**
I can identify ways of helping infants achieve self-regulation and develop coping skills.	☐	☐	☐
I can identify ways of helping young toddlers explore their world and make new discoveries without being destructive or wasteful and without causing injury to themselves or others.	☐	☐	☐
I can help older toddlers cope with fear, anger, and frustration and strike a balance between their longing for nurturance and desire to be independent.	☐	☐	☐
I know ways of helping preschool children recognize and value differences, resolve conflicts, express their feelings in words, and accept reasonable limits.	☐	☐	☐
I can recognize ways of using positive guidance techniques to reduce children's unwanted behaviors.	☐	☐	☐
I can provide positive guidance for children whose families use styles of discipline that are different from those I have been taught.	☐	☐	☐

GUIDANCE • Pretraining Personal Goal

Based on your pretraining self-assessment, write a personal goal for this Functional Area and an action plan describing how you will accomplish the goal.

Goal _____

_____

_____

_____

Action Plan _____

_____

_____

_____

_____

_____

_____

_____

_____

_____

_____

_____

_____

Save your goal and action plan for the end of this unit so you will be able to answer these questions: How did you accomplish your goal? And how has your behavior changed based on your training?

To identify ways of helping infants achieve self-regulation and develop coping skills

Separation and stranger anxiety are natural and appropriate in the first and second years of life. Infants demonstrate the development of an intimate relationship with a parent or caregiver when they protest to a new caregiver or show distress when a parent or caregiver leaves the room.

Mrs. G was really upset. She had always prided herself on being able to help children transition into a child care setting, but her best techniques were not working with Cedrik. She decided to write down everything that happened during drop-off time:

Mrs. L arrived at the child care center with 10-month-old Cedrik at 8:35 A.M. Most of the infants had already arrived. My assistant was changing a diaper, and I was watching three mobile infants who were in the play area. I greeted Mrs. L and held my arms out to Cedrik. Cedrik smiled and seemed happy to come with me until his mother asked him to give her one last good-bye kiss. As Cedrik's mother held him in her arms for the kiss, she addressed me in a somewhat stern voice, saying, "You will remember to change his diaper as soon as he gets wet, and be sure to warm his bottle just enough to get the chill off." Cedrik looked up at his mother, and his expression changed to a worried look. At this point, Mrs. L explained that she was late for work and placed Cedrik in my arms. Cedrik screamed as his mother left the center, and it took me a good 10 minutes to calm him down.

Explain to Cedrik's mother why the transition was hard.

_____

_____

_____

_____

_____

_____

Give her two ideas for making the transition easier.

1. _____

2. _____

To identify ways of helping young toddlers explore their world and make new discoveries without being destructive or wasteful and without causing injury to themselves or others

Many caregivers describe young toddlers as both the most fun and the most exhausting group of youngsters they have ever worked with. One minute, they find themselves laughing at a young toddler's antics, and the next minute, they are making a mad dash across the room in an attempt to prevent a calamity. Jeremy has just discovered the fun of opening and shutting the classroom door, or Victoria has discovered a hole in the beanbag chair and is about to swallow a bean.

Young toddlers have a way of finding safety hazards that no one else had ever discovered, of getting into things that were supposedly out of their reach, and of finding a novel way to use a toy, a piece of equipment, or the contents of their lunch box. A major task of caregivers of young toddlers is to find guidance techniques that preserve the children and the environment without robbing them of their zest for exploration and invention.

Miss Wet-Behind-the-Ears has been assigned as the assistant teacher to the class with eight 1- to 2-year-olds. The teacher has asked her to watch the children while she makes a phone call. Please help Miss Wet-Behind-the-Ears find some positive techniques for handling the following situations.

Hannah is standing on a low chair. She has just discovered that she can make the room get lighter and then darker by switching the light on and off. She is very proud of herself.

_____

_____

_____

Matthew is playing in the sensory bin that used to be filled with oatmeal. He is using one of the cardboard blocks as a scoop and has covered the floor with oatmeal.

_____

_____

_____

Juliet is riding with Horace in the rocking boat and keeps making it rock faster and faster. Horace is screaming, but Juliet won't stop long enough for him to get off.

_____

_____

_____

Anthony has managed to pull down his shorts and his training pants and is happily wetting the floor.

_____

_____

_____

Alberto is playing with Carmen and has bit her hand.

_____

_____

_____

To help older toddlers cope with fear, anger, and frustration and strike a balance between their longing for nurturance and desire to be independent

Two-year-olds present many challenges to their caregivers. At one moment, they recklessly climb up the ladder of a slide and need careful watching. At the next moment, they cling in fear to the caregiver because they heard a dog barking in the distance. Equally challenging for caregivers is the fact that 2-year-olds love to make choices but have difficulty making up their minds. It is not unlike a 2-year-old to ask for the red chair in a demanding voice and then declare with just as much force that he doesn't want the red chair. He wants the blue chair. While this kind of behavior may not be easy to cope with, it is typical 2-year-old behavior.

The 2-year-old is recognizing herself as a person who can make choices and assert her will. This new burst of autonomy is both exciting and scary, and it is not surprising that the 2-year-old sometimes falls apart and has what parents describe as a "meltdown."

Mrs. Hassled has just been changed from the infant to the 2-year-old classroom. She is having all kinds of problems and needs your help. Please give her some ideas for managing these situations.

Erica is screaming. Her cookie has broken in two pieces, and she wants it put back together.

_____

_____

_____

Pedro is having a full-blown temper tantrum. He wanted Maydie to change crayons with him. Mrs. Hassled managed to convince Maydie to exchange crayons, but now Pedro wants his own crayons back.

_____

_____

_____

Maria, who is usually a real daredevil, is hiding in the corner because Maureen brought her rabbit to school.

_____

_____

_____

To learn ways of helping preschool children recognize and value differences, resolve conflicts, express their feelings in words, and accept reasonable limits

Miss Letter-of-the-Law learned in school that it is important to help children learn to use words to express their feelings and assert their needs. She decided to try the technique in her class. In some situations, it has worked well. In other situations, it hasn't worked at all.

Identify the situations where the words Miss Letter-of-the-Law is using are almost certain not to work. What should she have done in these situations?

Petrinka scribbled on Arturo's artwork, and Arturo scratched her in response. Miss Letter-of the-Law held Arturo's hand and said, "Arturo, scratching is not allowed. I know you were angry when Petrinka wrote on your paper, but you need to tell her in words. Say, 'Petrinka, don't scribble on my paper.' "

Angelina, age 2, bit Portia on the arm. Miss Letter-of-the-Law put Angelina on her knee. "Angelina, I know you wanted the dinosaur that Portia was playing with, but biting is not allowed. Next time, ask her if you can please have a turn with the dinosaur."

Cavendish had been in a bad mood all morning. At lunchtime, he pushed three children out of his way and got in front of the line. Miss Letter-of-the-Law looked at him sternly. "Cavendish, I know you are feeling upset today, but you do not push and shove children. Next time say, 'Please move. I want to be in the front of the line.' "

Objective 5
To recognize ways of using positive guidance techniques to reduce children's unwanted behaviors

Children come to understand what behavior is acceptable when limits are clearly and positively defined. The consistent response of caregivers to infants helps them develop a basic trust in the environment that supports their response to positive guidance as they grow. As toddlers struggle to become independent, adults can respect their experiments with asserting "No!" and can encourage self-reliance while maintaining clear limits.

Mrs. Rigid was bringing her group of 1- to 2-year-olds in from the play area. When she asked 18-month-old Vicki if she was ready to come inside, Vicki shouted "No." Mrs. Rigid responded sharply, "Yes you are, because it's time to go in" and moved Vicki, now crying, over to the door.

How could Mrs. Rigid have better handled this situation?

_____

_____

Creating Classroom Guidelines

"Do you have a set of classroom rules?" the evaluator asked Mrs. Wilson. Mrs. Wilson answered proudly, "Oh, yes. I have them listed there on the wall. We go over them every morning."

Sure enough, on the wall was a long sheet of brown paper with the following rules written on it:

> NO biting.
>
> NO kicking.
>
> NO fighting.
>
> NO knocking down other children's block constructions.
>
> NO throwing blocks.
>
> NO going out barefoot on the playground.
>
> NO walking behind the swings.
>
> NO messing up the room.
>
> NO throwing food around.
>
> NO getting off your mat at naptime.

The evaluator seemed displeased.

What is wrong with this list? Help Mrs. Wilson develop a more appropriate list of guidelines.

1. _____

2. _____

3. _____

4. _____

5. _____

Competency Goal III • To support social and emotional development and provide positive guidance

Even if Mrs. Wilson's list had been more appropriate, the idea of going over a whole set of rules daily is not a practical one. Wherever possible, teach a rule in context. In other words, if there is a rule about the playground, talk about the rule as you go out to the playground. If there is a rule about cleaning up after lunch, the right time to talk about it is at lunchtime. Children can remember quite a few rules if the rules make sense to them and they are learned in the appropriate contexts. The more the children understand, the more they will comply.

In addition, when developing rules for the classroom, remember the following points:

1. Rules should be easily understood.
2. Rules should be stated clearly and positively.
3. Rules should be short and concise.
4. Older children should be involved in the development of classroom rules.

Recognizing Ways of Helping Children Become Self-Directive

Miss Namby-Pamby loved children and tried very hard to be a good teacher. The one problem that she seemed to have was that the children in her class had a tendency to become overly active. By the end of the day, the classroom was usually in a shambles and the children out of sorts. Mr. Spotter, the director of the preschool, decided to observe her classroom. Here are the notes he made:

8:15 Miss Namby-Pamby announced to the children that it was circle time. She took attendance and then told the children that it was time for rhythm band. She gave the children their instruments and then went to the back of the room to look for the music CD. By the time she got back, Helena and Alberto were arguing about who had the drum first.

10:00 Activity time. Gina and Korinne were playing "firefighter" and accidentally knocked down Trevor's jet port, which he had built in the middle of the floor.

10:30 Art time. Hitesh is having a temper tantrum because everyone else got to make a shadow box and there were no boxes left for him.

11:00   Clean-up time. Miss Namby-Pamby is trying to put away the puzzles because none of the children admit to messing them up.

12:00   Lunchtime. Brigette stands on the table, and everybody's lunch and juice land on the floor.

1:30   Naptime. A palmetto bug crawls on Gina's mat, and three children start screaming. Miss Namby-Pamby says she is afraid of cockroaches, so I stop taking notes and put an end to the bug.

Help Miss Namby-Pamby identify six changes that she should make in her classroom arrangements and procedures.

1. _____

2. _____

3. _____

4. _____

5. _____

6. _____

Organizing Your Center to Facilitate Guidance

Following are suggestions for organizing your center more effectively. After each, indicate any additional suggestions you have or special ways that you accomplish the same goal.

1. *Dividing the space*   Low shelves, dividers, tables, and cloth hangings can be used to create cozy areas where small groups of children can play uninterrupted.

   _____

   _____

   _____

   _____

   _____

2. *Arranging the room* The better the job that we do in arranging the classroom, the easier it is to keep things in order. Clean-up time is both more enjoyable and less time consuming when the children can see at a glance where every item belongs. When the shelves in an interest center are coded by color, shape, or symbol, the task of cleaning up is in itself a learning experience.

_____

_____

_____

_____

3. *Being prepared ahead of time* A good teacher walks through the day mentally before the first child arrives. What materials are needed for the group activities, for individual activities, for snacktime, and for assessment? If everything is on hand and organized, the day goes so much more smoothly. Children are not very good at waiting. Time spent looking for things to begin an activity is double the time spent. Inevitably, the teacher has to spend extra time recapturing the attention of the children.

_____

_____

_____

_____

4. *Developing signals* There are many different ways of signaling clean-up time and preparing children to move to a new activity. One of the most effective ways is to use a special song. When the children hear the music, they know that they have just a few minutes to get their things back on the shelf and move to the next activity.

_____

_____

_____

_____

5. *Helping children help themselves* The more children can do for themselves, the more smoothly your preschool classroom will run and the easier it will be to move into new activities. You can help children become more self-sufficient in these ways:

- Make sure that the children have their own personal cubbies to keep their own things.
- Make sure that the children can name and identify all the interest centers in your classroom.
- Help the children learn to help themselves to classroom supplies and materials.
- Teach the children to use the toilet, wash their hands, and brush their teeth.
- Teach the children where the trash is and what sorts of things belong in the trash.

Add two additional suggestions to the list:

1. _____

   _____

2. _____

   _____

6. *Optimizing time that is spent waiting in line or moving from place to place* Every early childhood teacher should have her own special "bag of tricks" to use during transition periods. The bag of tricks should include techniques for the following:

- Getting children's attention quickly
- Calming a classroom when the children are overexcited
- Minimizing waiting time
- Moving the class from one place to another
- Making routine activities productive learning experiences

Describe your bag of tricks for accomplishing two of these challenges:

1. _____

   _____

2. _____

   _____

We have talked so far about ways to engineer a classroom that will minimize the amount of conflict and disruptive behavior. Yet we all know that in even the best-run classrooms, some children will act out some of the time. Knowing positive guidance and discipline methods is critical for every child and teacher.

Mrs. Almost-But-Not-Quite took a course in positive ways to discipline and developed her own set of guidelines for maintaining a classroom:

1. *Anticipate:* Don't wait for trouble to happen. Recognize warning signs and diffuse behavior that could cause trouble. If two children are occupying the swing set, divert the class bully who is headed in that direction.

2. *Redirect:* When a child is engaged in antisocial behavior, provide her with a positive suggestion for a new and more appropriate activity.

3. *Reinforce:* Reinforce positive behavior. Catch children being good. If you praise children when they behave in an appropriate way, they are likely to increase this behavior.

4. *Share:* Share the task of setting rules and limits with the children. Children are more likely to follow rules that they have helped create.

5. *Restate rule:* The simplest and often the most effective way to resolve conflict or change negative behavior is simply to restate the rule.

6. *Ignore:* Ignore negative behavior, if no harm or danger is involved. Children sometimes act up for attention, and if you don't pay attention to the behavior, it is more likely to disappear.

7. *Positive practice:* Positive practice is helpful in some situations. The child who hits another child could practice doing something helpful for the victim, like helping her put away her toys.

8. *Encourage using words:* With a little help, children can learn to express their negative feelings with words, rather than actions.

9. *Provide choices:* When a child wants a toy that another child is playing with, bring her two other toys and let her choose the one she wants to play with.

Mrs. Almost-But-Not-Quite posted her list on the bulletin board so that the other staff members could share it. Just as she was doing so, she heard some screaming from her class. She hurried in to find Imogene snatching a Power Rangers figure out of Arthur's hand.

"I can't trust you kids for a second. All I do is turn my back, and you kids are at each other's throats. You know the rules of the classroom! No fighting, no standing on tables, and any toy you don't want to share stays in the cubby. It's downright embarrassing to have you act up this way. Now, do you want to have playground time, or do you want to spend the day in time-out?"

Obviously, poor Mrs. Almost-But-Not-Quite needs your help. Using her own list of guidelines, explain to Mrs. Almost-But-Not-Quite how she could have handled the situation more effectively.

_____

_____

_____

_____

_____

To recognize ways of providing positive guidance for children whose families use styles of discipline that are different from those the teacher has been taught

Early childhood training courses like this focus on taking a preventive approach to guiding children's behavior. Children need many opportunities to learn to behave. They learn best when teachers give them positive attention and praise for doing right while downplaying negative outbursts. However, not all families have adopted this approach.

Practitioners sometimes have to find a difficult balance between respecting parents' points of view and being true to their own knowledge about positive guidance. Sometimes, a teacher can use humor to get around a parent's inappropriate demand. Other times, the teacher may have to explain why she does not use physical punishment, attempting to clearly state the reasons for a positive approach that teaches rather than punishes the child. Other times, the teacher has to change her behavior after listening to the parent's point of view. The important thing is to keep the needs of the child in mind while being open to other points of view and keeping the lines of communication open with the parents.

Mrs. Sharp-Tongue was talking with her child's teacher. "When Morris whines, I want you to cut it short with a little swat to his behind. Sometimes, you just have to surprise him."

Help Morris's teacher respond to Mrs. Sharp-Tongue's demand.

_____

_____

_____

_____

_____

_____

_____

_____

GUIDANCE • *Observation Opportunity*

Name _____

Observe a caregiver with toddlers or preschool children for up to 20 minutes. Write a narrative report of a teacher/child interaction in which the teacher used some form of positive or negative guidance. Describe exactly what happened without providing an interpretation.

_____

_____

_____

_____

_____

_____

_____

_____

_____

_____

_____

_____

_____

_____

_____

_____

_____

_____

_____

GUIDANCE • Challenge Activities

Name _____

Challenge 1

Describe at least one way that you have used each of these positive guidance strategies in your setting.

1. Anticipate: _____

_____

2. Redirect: _____

_____

3. Reinforce a positive behavior: _____

_____

4. Restate rule: _____

_____

5. Ignore negative behavior: _____

_____

6. Positive practice: _____

_____

7. Encourage using words: _____

_____

8. Provide choices: _____

_____

9. Other? _____

_____

Challenge 2

Describe how you prepare for the transitions in your day. You may use your basic schedule/routine as a guideline.

Time	Activity	Description of transition from one activity to next

GUIDANCE • Post-Training Wrap-Up

After completing this unit, review your personal goal and action plan and describe how you accomplished your goal.

_____

_____

_____

_____

List at least three ways in which you changed your behavior as a result of your training in this Functional Area.

1. _____

2. _____

3. _____

GUIDANCE • Professional Resource File

Resource Items

Collect the items for the Professional Resource File related to this Functional Area (if applicable). Refer to the pages at the back of this *Trainee's Manual* (pp. 281–283) and to the CDA booklet from the Council for Professional Recognition for specific instructions.

Statement of Competence

Write a short essay of 75 to 150 words, listing one or more goals you have for yourself and for the children and families in the area of Guidance and describing activities you do to achieve these goals. Describe your experiences in your own words. Be concise. Use "I" statements—for example, "To help children develop a sense of self-direction, I pose the rules for class guidance as positive statements, and I set up opportunities for children to make choices."

For additional information about writing your Statement of Competence, refer to the workbook section at the end of this *Trainee's Manual* (pp. 283–312) and to the CDA booklet from the Council for Professional Recognition.

The statements you have written for the chapters Self, Social, and Guidance together make up the Competency Goal Statement for Goal III: To support social and emotional development and to provide positive guidance.

Chapter 11

Families

Overview

In the context of child care, the *family* can be defined as the person or people who have primary responsibility for the care, nurturing, and upbringing of the child. The family is the crucible for transmitting culture, heritage, and traditions across the generations.

Today's families come in many forms: one or two parents and their children; adoptive, blended, step-, and foster families; families with two fathers or two mothers; and multigenerational extended families. When the word *parent* is used in this chapter, it means anyone who fills this role. When we talk about *families*, we mean to embrace their diversity. We recognize that in many cultures, parents, grandparents, and other relatives are all involved in making decisions about children's welfare. It is important for teachers and caregivers to get to know the whole family, however it is defined.

Rationale

It is widely believed that parents are, and in general should be, the single most important influence on the education and development of their children. It is the role of the teacher to maximize the impact of the educational experience by involving the parents and families in the life of the school or center. By encouraging involvement, by communicating frequently, by offering opportunities for input, and by exchanging information, the teacher creates an atmosphere of cooperation that benefits the child, her family, and the school or center.

Objectives

Objective 1 To understand the many purposes of establishing good communication with parents

Objective 2 To learn how to set up a parent/school partnership

Objective 3 To learn strategies for keeping parents informed about center activities and encouraging participation in parent meetings and volunteer opportunities

Objective 4 To learn strategies for serving as a resource for families and building a community that supports families

Objective 5 To learn strategies for engaging parents in decision making and advocacy

FAMILIES • Pretest

Complete each of the following items as indicated.

1. List three ways families can participate in your child care setting.

   a. _____

   b. _____

   c. _____

2. Put an "X" in front of each statement that suggests a good way of conducting a parent conference.

   _____ a. Call the parents the day before a scheduled conference to confirm the time and the date.

   _____ b. Gather and organize samples of the child's work to share with her parents.

   _____ c. Make a list ahead of time of all the things you would like to tell the parents. When you complete the list, ask the parents if they have any questions.

   _____ d. Be sure to answer any phone calls during the meeting. You want parents to think you are always available.

   _____ e. Be sure that the meeting takes place where the parents are comfortable and there is privacy, so they can talk freely about their child.

3. The best time to have a parent conference is:

   _____ a. in the morning.

   _____ b. in the evening.

   _____ c. at a time mutually convenient for you and the family.

   _____ d. on the weekend.

   _____ e. Why bother with meetings? The parents don't care anyway.

4. Why is cooperation between home and school important?

   _____

   _____

FAMILIES • Self-Assessment

Indicate how you feel about your skills and abilities in each of the following categories by checking the appropriate column.

	Pretraining		
	Strong	**Satisfactory**	**Needs Improvement**
I understand the many purposes of establishing good communication with parents.	☐	☐	☐
I know how to set up a parent/school partnership.	☐	☐	☐
I know strategies for keeping parents informed about center activities and encouraging participation in parent meetings and volunteer opportunities.	☐	☐	☐
I know strategies for serving as a resource for families and building a community that supports families.	☐	☐	☐
I know strategies for engaging parents in decision making and advocacy.	☐	☐	☐

FAMILIES • Pretraining Personal Goal

Based on your pretraining self-assessment, write a personal goal for this Functional Area and an action plan describing how you will accomplish the goal.

Goal _____

_____

_____

_____

Action Plan _____

_____

_____

_____

_____

_____

_____

_____

_____

_____

_____

_____

Save your goal and action plan for the end of this unit so you will be able to answer these questions: How did you accomplish your goal? And how has your behavior changed based on your training?

Competency Goal IV • To establish positive and productive relationships with families

To understand the many purposes of establishing good communication with parents

Communication includes both sending out and receiving information. Sometimes in dealing with parents, we have difficulty making sure that information flows in both directions.

On the one hand, we have parents who come on strong. These parents have set ideas about what they want for their children. Parent conferences turn out to be monologues, and we get no opportunity either to ask questions or to provide information. More frequently, we find ourselves in the opposite situation. The parents sit by quietly while we tell them all about their child and end up learning nothing. But again, we say to ourselves, "Things could be worse." Somehow, the parents we want to see the most are the ones who seem never to spend time at the center.

Obviously, we cannot rely solely on the formal parent/teacher conference to set up communication with parents. Our relationships with the parents of our children must be treasured, and we need to nurture these relationships in as many ways as we can.

We have many different ways of establishing communication with parents:

1. Home visits
2. Parent/teacher conferences
3. Telephone calls
4. Parent advisory board meetings
5. Parent education meetings
6. Open houses
7. Children's performances
8. Letters
9. Notes in the child's backpack
10. Center newsletters
11. Parent bulletin boards
12. Poster of daily events by entrance

Add two items to this list.

1. _____

2. _____

It is important for us as caregivers to recognize the benefits of establishing good rapport with our parents:

1. The parents can provide us with information about their child that will help us understand him better.

2. By getting a feel for the child's home life, we can gain insight into her reactions to the child care center environment. If we have a child who is shy and withdrawn, for instance, it helps us to know that the child comes from a home where she is a well-protected only child.

3. By meeting with parents, we have the opportunity of making sure that the home and center share common objectives for the child's development and that the value systems are congruent. If the center, on the one hand, is teaching a child not to fight and the home encourages fighting back, the child will be caught in the middle and left confused as to what is the appropriate way to behave.

4. By getting the parents interested in what the child is learning, we can encourage them to reinforce those emerging skills at home.

5. Contact with the parents serves to remind us that we teach the child for a fleeting year. The child will not even likely remember us, but the parents will be influencing the child throughout the formative years. The parents are the child's real teachers, and we are at best only substitutes. When we share our expertise with the child's parents, we extend our influence into the child's future.

Assuming that we agree on the importance of contact with parents, we will now turn our attention to finding ways of making our own contacts with parents a mutually rewarding experience.

A group of Head Start teachers attending a regional meeting were discussing their ideas for encouraging the involvement of parents in the education of their children:

Mrs. Cooper: "In our school, we have divided the children among the staff. Every staff member is responsible for making at least one contact per month with the parents on her list."

Mrs. Warner: "I have always believed in home visits. If I go out of my way to visit every home, the whole year goes well."

Mrs. Jones: "In our center, we have found that the secret to good meetings is planning. There are two facets to good planning. First, we always plan before a parent meeting: What do we want to tell our parents? What do we want to show our parents? What do we want to find out about the child? What would we like the parents to do? Second, we always plan for the meeting itself. We call or send a note home the night before to remind the parents of the meeting. We arrange our time so that our full attention can focus on the parents. Also, we make sure that we have on hand all the papers and crafts we want to show the parents, so that we won't waste valuable time looking for things."

Mrs. Clark: "In our school, we have a parent file. We write down every time we make contact with a parent—what it was about and the outcome of the contact. You'd be surprised how useful this file can be."

Miss Beckford: "We started something this year that seems to work really well. We have a weekly newspaper called *Parents* that we send home with the children. It's only a page and doesn't take long to do. This gives us an opportunity to recognize parents who make a contribution to the center, to congratulate parents on their birthdays, and to keep parents informed about school events.

Now it's your turn. Assume that you are attending this meeting and add two ideas of your own.

1. _____

   _____

   _____

   _____

2. _____

   _____

   _____

   _____

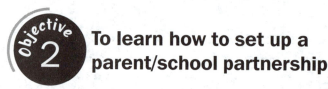

To learn how to set up a parent/school partnership

We must recognize that no matter how hard we try, we will never be the child's most influential teachers. The information we provide for parents in the area of child development is probably just as important as our interactions with the children.

Parent meetings are usually the best place to provide information on child growth and development. It works best if you can use videos or other visual aids to spark up the meeting. Also, there are some very fine commercially available programs that can be used to give parents a background in child growth and development and to suggest effective parenting techniques.

Although it is important to share effective child-rearing techniques with parents, there is also a danger: Child-rearing techniques are largely determined by our parents' parenting style, which in turn reflects our culturally based beliefs and values. In order to remain respectful to different cultures, we need to focus child-rearing discussions on problems or concerns identified by parents and invite other parents to suggest alternative ways of dealing with their concerns.

Miss Wood is very uneasy about her first parent meeting. This is her first year in a child care center, and she feels that she lacks the information and experience to offer advice to parents.

In order to help her, you are assembling a list of the most common parental concerns and questions. In addition, you will make suggestions regarding the most appropriate responses. After each of the questions listed, indicate how you feel Miss Wood should respond.

If my child bites, should I bite her back?

_____

_____

My 2-year-old refuses to share her toys. What should I do about it?

_____

_____

My child is always being picked on. Should I teach him how to fight back?

_____

_____

My 4-year-old tells lies. Should I wash her mouth out with soap?

_____

_____

Should I let my kid hit me? How do you handle scratching and hair pulling?

_____

_____

Since the new baby came, my older child wants to be a baby. What do I do?

_____

_____

My 4-year-old still wets his bed. How should I punish him?

_____

_____

My toddler doesn't sleep through the night. What should I do?

_____

_____

Good work! Now add two or three additional questions, including the possible answers.

1. _____

_____

_____

2. _____

   _____

   _____

3. _____

   _____

   _____

To learn strategies for keeping parents informed about center activities and encouraging participation in parent meetings and volunteer opportunities

Mrs. Baxter, the new center director, overheard some of her teachers discussing parent involvement. These were some of their comments:

> "All my parents work."
>
> "My parents don't have transportation."
>
> "It takes more time telling parents what to do than doing it myself."
>
> "Most of my parents don't really care."

Mrs. Baxter was dismayed. No matter how hard she could try, she knew that she couldn't dispute some of the reasons that teachers have for not using parents as volunteers. It is hard work enlisting parent volunteers, and it can be a source of frustration.

But Mrs. Baxter wouldn't give up. She decided on the following three-pronged approach, to be worked out first and then presented to the teaching staff:

1. *Provide many different kinds of opportunities for parents to help.* We must recognize that all parents who work outside the home do not work all the time. If we are creative in the types of opportunities we provide for parents to contribute to the class, we can overcome the problem of the working parent.

List five ways for parents to use their skills and talents for your center.

1. _____

2. _____

3. _____

4. _____

5. _____

2. *Make the very best use of parents when they do volunteer.* There is nothing more frustrating to a parent than to give up a morning to come into the classroom and find herself standing around with nothing to do.

List three ways of making sure that parents' time is not wasted.

1. _____

2. _____

3. _____

3. *Recognize parents for their contributions.* Everyone likes recognition. If we find creative ways of thanking parents for the contributions they make to the classroom, they are more likely to volunteer again.

List three ways of recognizing parents for the contributions they make.

1. _____

2. _____

3. _____

To learn strategies for serving as a resource for families and building a community that supports families

Mrs. Down-to-Business kept her communications with parents short and to the point.

When Johnnie's mother asked if she could help her find a clinic that provided free vaccinations, her response was "Sorry, but I don't know of any."

When Violetta's mother asked if there were parks in the neighborhood where she could bring Violetta after school, Mrs. Down-to-Business said that Violetta had plenty of time to play on the school playground and didn't need a park.

When Jeremy's mother talked about how much Jeremy loved music and asked if there were any children's concerts he could go to, Mrs. Down-to-Business told her that Jeremy was too young to go to concerts.

The preschool director overheard Mrs. Down-to-Business's responses to parents and asked her to think about a better way to respond to the parents' questions.

Please help Mrs. Down-to-Business by providing an appropriate answer for each of the questions she was asked.

1. _____

_____

_____

_____

2. _____

_____

_____

_____

3. _____

_____

_____

_____

To learn strategies for engaging parents in decision making and advocacy

Once you have opened up channels of communication with parents, maintain that good communication in these ways:

1. Set up regular parent conferences related to the child's progress.
2. Use the telephone as a means of sharing information.
3. Use the mail or the children to send home information.
4. Involve parents in a variety of ways in classroom activities.
5. Hold parent meetings that are both interesting and informative.

You have already put in place the mechanism for keeping parents informed about what is happening at the center. But don't limit your communication to major events. Let your parents know about the small things that are happening: having a visit from area firefighters, making popcorn, blowing bubbles on the playground, and making classroom projects. Parents can then discuss these things with their children at home.

Another form of parent participation is the parent advisory or action group. This may be a particular plus for your center. You are more apt to achieve a useful level of parent participation if you inform parents as to the following:

1. What is the parent advisory or action group for?
2. Who are the members of the group?
3. How often do they meet?
4. Where do they meet?
5. What kinds of things do they accomplish?
6. What are the benefits of serving in the group?

Make out a fact sheet for parents answering these questions. Include any additional information that you think is important.

_____

_____

_____

_____

_____

FAMILIES • *Observation Opportunity*

Name _____

Attend a parent advisory group, PTA, or action group in an early child-hood setting. List the topics that were discussed. Why do you think these topics were important to the group?

Group observed: _____

Date: _____   **Time:** _____

Topics:	**Importance to group:**
1. _____	_____
_____	_____
_____	_____
2. _____	_____
_____	_____
_____	_____
3. _____	_____
_____	_____
_____	_____

Other observations:

_____

_____

_____

_____

_____

FAMILIES • Challenge Activities

Name _____

Challenge 1

Write an article for a parent newsletter that includes a paragraph on how children learn through play. For example, describe what children are learning when they engage in dramatic play.

_____

_____

_____

_____

_____

_____

_____

_____

_____

_____

_____

_____

_____

_____

_____

_____

_____

_____

_____

_____

_____

Challenge 2

Create two mock bulletin boards. One should be a parent-to-parent bulletin board, where parents can exchange information with each other. The second should be a teacher-to-parent bulletin board, where you describe planned classroom activities, announce upcoming parent events, and ask for donations like recycled materials.

Parent-to-Parent Bulletin Board

Teacher-to-Parent Bulletin Board

FAMILIES • Post-Training Assessment

After completing this unit, review your personal goal and action plan and describe how you accomplished your goal.

_____

_____

_____

_____

List at least three ways in which you changed your behavior as a result of your training in this Functional Area.

1. _____

2. _____

3. _____

FAMILIES • Professional Resource File

Resource Items

Collect the items for the Professional Resource File related to this Functional Area (if applicable). Refer to the pages at the back of this *Trainee's Manual* (pp. 281–283) and to the CDA booklet from the Council for Professional Recognition for specific instructions.

Statement of Competence

Write an essay of 200 to 500 words, listing one or more goals you have for yourself and for the children and families in the area of Families and describing activities you do to achieve these goals. Describe your experiences in your own words. Be concise. Use "I" statements—for example, "I make sure that every parent is greeted when he or she comes into our program, and I try to make parents feel comfortable staying a few minutes to play with their child before they need to leave for work."

For additional information about writing your Statement of Competence, refer to the workbook section at the end of this *Trainee's Manual* (pp. 283–312) and to the CDA booklet from the Council for Professional Recognition.

Program Management

Overview

Program management in child care refers to the role of the teachers in promoting the smooth running of the child care center. It includes observing, recording, and tracking the development and behavior of each child; following administrative policies and procedures set by the center; working as a team with other members of the staff in program and curriculum planning; and participating with the director and other staff members in evaluating the strengths and needs of the center. In family child care, program management includes curriculum planning, record keeping, business management, and other administrative duties.

Rationale

The level of cooperation evidenced by staff members is a critical component in the development of a healthy, productive center. In the best of circumstances, staff members share resources, materials, and ideas. In addition, time is set aside for joint planning and problem solving. Staff meetings are devoted to discussing problems and identifying opportunities.

Being a good program manager requires both interpersonal skills and managerial skills. The teacher with program management skills can work cooperatively with other teachers, sharing ideas, resources, and expertise. In addition, a good program manager is able to maintain individual records on all of the children in her class and use these records as the basis for program planning and curriculum development.

Objectives

- **Objective 1**   To work cooperatively as a member of a team

- **Objective 2**   To follow the policies and procedures set down by the center

- **Objective 3**   To maintain a record-keeping system that serves as the basis for individual and group program planning

- **Objective 4**   To manage a classroom efficiently so that most of the teacher's time can be devoted to working directly with the children

PROGRAM MANAGEMENT • Pretest

Choose the most appropriate item to complete each statement.

_____ 1. Anecdotal records are:

    a. used by most parents.

    b. used to keep track of immunizations.

    c. written records used to describe significant behaviors.

    d. no longer used because they are old fashioned.

_____ 2. Record keeping is necessary for:

    a. the teacher.

    b. the aide.

    c. the director.

    d. All of the above

_____ 3. Activity plans are important because:

    a. they help the staff think through the purpose of an activity.

    b. they provide an opportunity to think through the steps of an activity.

    c. they describe the materials that will be needed for an activity.

    d. they provide a permanent record of group activities.

    e. All of the above

_____ 4. Materials used in the classroom should always be:

    a. selected from a good early childhood catalog.

    b. teacher-made.

    c. developmentally appropriate for the children in the class.

    d. self-corrective.

Give four reasons staff meetings are valuable.

1. _____

2. _____

3. _____

4. _____

Suggest one strategy for finding a time and place to have a planning meeting with your co-workers.

_____

_____

_____

_____

_____

_____

_____

PROGRAM MANAGEMENT • Self-Assessment

Indicate how you feel about your skills and abilities in each of the following categories by checking the appropriate column.

	Pretraining		
	Strong	**Satisfactory**	***Needs Improvement***
I can work cooperatively as a member of a team.	☐	☐	☐
I can follow the policies and procedures set down by the center.	☐	☐	☐
I can maintain a record-keeping system that serves as the basis for individual and group program planning.	☐	☐	☐
I can manage a classroom efficiently so that most of my time can be devoted to working directly with the children.	☐	☐	☐

PROGRAM MANAGEMENT • Pretraining Personal Goal

Based on your pretraining self-assessment, write a personal goal for this Functional Area and an action plan describing how you will accomplish the goal.

Goal _____

_____

_____

_____

Action Plan _____

_____

_____

_____

_____

_____

_____

_____

_____

_____

_____

_____

_____

Save your goal and action plan for the end of this unit so you will be able to answer these questions: How did you accomplish your goal? And how has your behavior changed based on your training?

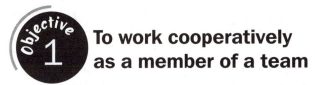

To work cooperatively as a member of a team

In previous units, we have discussed many of the important aspects of creating and maintaining a supportive and facilitative experience for children. But no matter how beautifully equipped, how well organized, or how sound the policies, if the staff of the center cannot work together harmoniously, the success of the entire effort will be greatly diminished.

As you work through this unit, keep in mind the following six criteria for a cooperative staff:

1. Each person carries her share of the load.
2. Staff members are capable and willing to assist each other, if the need arises.
3. Planning is a joint enterprise, and staff members voluntarily agree to share in the work associated with a special event.
4. Minor problems are discussed before they grow into major ones.
5. Staff members share their ideas, their talents, and their concerns.
6. Staff members show mutual trust and concern for each other.

Now read the following transcript of a staff meeting of the Ding-Dong Preschool:

Director: "Tell me about the field trip to the farm. How did everything go?"

Teacher 1: "It was great fun. We got to see the nursery where the baby lambs are born."

Teacher 2: "Even the bus ride there and back was fun. Both classes practiced the same songs: "Old McDonald Had a Farm," "Mary Had a Little Lamb," and "The Wheels on the Bus." The children had fun singing together."

Teacher 1: "And the idea about the animal nametags worked so well. Each child in both of our classes cut out an animal tag the day before, and we put the center's name on it. Before the field trip, each child found his partner from the other class—the "lamb" in my class found someone with a "lamb" in Delphine's class. This way, each child got to have a buddy and make a new friend."

Director: "It sounds great. Did you have any follow-up activities?"

Teacher 1: "Oh, yes. Delphine went to the library and got two farm animal books that we shared for reading time, and I got some cartons and boxes from the supermarket and each class made a farm model."

Director: "Why do you think it worked so well this time?"

Teacher 2: "Do you want to know the truth?"

Director: "Of course."

Teacher 2: "Well, we didn't invite Jeanette to bring her class. It never works when her class comes along because she's just not with it."

Director: "What do you mean 'not with it?' "

Teacher 1: "You know, she is such a scatterbrain! When we went on the picnic, she was supposed to bring the bug spray and she forgot. And when it was her turn to go to the library at Halloween, she brought back real dumb books that the children hated."

Please help the director from Ding-Dong Preschool. Which of the criteria for a cooperative staff does the Ding-Dong Preschool meet?

_____

_____

_____

_____

Provide three suggestions for improving staff cooperation at the Ding-Dong Preschool.

1. _____

    _____

2. _____

    _____

3. _____

    _____

To follow the policies and procedures set down by the center

Miss Go-with-the-Flow was working in the Collegiate Preschool. She knew that she was supposed to teach the children how to recognize letters and their associated sounds by holding up flash cards during circle time. Then she was supposed to go around the class and ask each child to name the letter and tell her a word that begins with that letter ("A" is for *apple*).

Miss Go-with-the-Flow knew many playful ways to introduce children to letters and she was very much against using flash cards. She was trying to decide what to do.

Help Miss Go-with-the-Flow by putting an "X" by each response that would be appropriate.

_____ I will put the flash cards on the top shelf and use them only when the director walks into the room.

_____ I will tell the director that her ideas about teaching are out of date and that she should read some of the newer literature.

_____ I will ask the director to put me in the class with the babies and let someone else worry about teaching the 4-year-olds their letters.

_____ I could hold a parents meeting and convince the parents that they don't want their children to be drilled and that they should complain to the director.

_____ I could explain to the director that she and I differ in our philosophy of teaching and that at the end of the year, I will seek a position in a school that is compatible with my philosophy.

_____ I could meet with the director and explain my philosophy for introducing prereading skills without flash cards.

To maintain a record-keeping system that serves as the basis for individual and group program planning

The greatest challenge that teachers of young children face is *individualization*. Individualization doesn't mean that each child is off working by himself with his own individual prescription. Rather, it means that when a child either selects or is presented with an activity, it is appropriate for his developmental level.

A superb teacher individualizes the curriculum by doing the following:

- Placing curriculum materials in the classroom that are varied and developmentally sequenced
- Arranging the classroom so that children have easy access to materials and can return them to the right places when they finish with them
- Observing every child carefully and keeping a written record of the skills she has achieved
- Developing a daily schedule that allows children to work both in small groups and individually
- Making weekly plans that provide each child opportunities to reinforce her emerging skills and acquire new ones

Obviously, record keeping is critical for every classroom teacher. Without good records, we cannot see where we've been or plan where we want to go.

Let us look at all the ways that records on individual children are used:

1. Records tell us how much progress all the children in the class have made. This tells us how effective our curriculum has been.

2. Records provide us with information on the progress of each individual child. Is the program right for her? Does she need individual help or referrals?

3. Records provide a basis for individual planning. Plans that are developed from individual records that indicate the skills a child has mastered are especially useful when a volunteer or classroom aide wants to work with her.

4. Records are extremely useful in communicating with parents and other staff members.

One form of record keeping that is a valuable tool for planning is a *challenge chart*.

Analyze the categories on the following chart to determine whether it would be useful to you. What categories would you add to make it better? Would it be useful to add a column "Evaluation of Success" to help you determine whether you would want to use this lesson plan another year or whether changes should be made?

Child's Name _____

Date	Areas of Developmental Concern	Planning Activities	Outcome

Use this blank chart to create your own challenge chart.

Child's Name _____

To manage a classroom efficiently so that most of the teacher's time can be devoted to working directly with the children

Managing a classroom efficiently requires both good organizational skills and at least one or two years of experience. It is difficult to know how to order materials and equipment, how to arrange the classroom, maintain resource files, and take advantage of volunteer helpers until you have had enough experience to know what works best for you. Once you have developed these organizational skills, you will discover that planning ahead is much easier, that you are spending less time searching for things, that you are much more relaxed, and that you have plenty of time to spend with the children.

Ordering and Gathering Materials

Very few teachers have the luxury of ordering everything for the classroom that they would really like to have. Seasoned teachers discover soon enough that the best way to ensure having an adequate supply of materials is to become a good scavenger. Whether you live in an urban area or a rural area, it is not too difficult to find sources of recycled materials that you can put to good use. Teacher-made materials that have been created from recyclables have many advantages:

- Children have a special feeling for materials that they know their teacher has created.
- If a part breaks, you can replace it.
- Teacher-made materials are created with an objective in mind and are used to achieve that objective.
- Teacher-made materials can easily be designed with a self-corrective element.
- Teacher-made materials get an immediate field test and are easy to redesign on the basis of feedback.

One of the most creative challenges for the teacher is to look at common, everyday objects and transform them into important instructional materials.

Here's a list of everyday objects that can be found in most communities.

Milk cartons	Paper towel spindles	Fabric samples
Buttons	Fruit or vegetable trays	Wallpaper samples
Playing cards	Catalogs	Flexible wire
Greeting cards	Shoeboxes	Paper plates
Yarn	Carpet squares	Clothespins
Paper bags	Egg cartons	Juice containers

Choose three objects from the list. Then use your creativity, imagination, and experience to indicate how you would modify or use each object to meet an instructional goal. Also, state the goal for your group of children. Good luck!

Item	**Game or Activity**	**Instructional Goal**
1. _____	_____	_____
_____	_____	_____
2. _____	_____	_____
_____	_____	_____
3. _____	_____	_____
_____	_____	_____

Organizing Your Classroom

How well you can organize your classroom has a lot to do with the amount of shelving and cabinets at your disposal. But even if you have limited furnishings, there are guidelines you can follow:

- Identify one shelf where you can keep all the things that you use on a daily basis.
- Place all the items that you will need to implement your weekly plan on a second shelf.
- Keep all items that you don't want children to access on a high shelf (for instance, large containers of paint).

- Keep all the special lists you need—like emergency telephone numbers, fire drill routes, and lists of child allergies—on a special bulletin board.
- Store materials and toys that you do not use on a daily basis in well-marked cabinets or boxes.
- Once you have decided how to arrange the classroom so that the children have easy access to books and toys, create visual cues so that the children will be able to participate in clean-up time, such as pictures, shape stickers, and stickers of different colors.

Describe the system you are using to make sure that the children can return toys and materials to the proper places.

_____

_____

Creating Resource Files

Resource files with plenty of room for additions are a necessary investment. Even when you have finished your CDA or early childhood courses, having a well-organized resource file will be a vital time saver.

Describe the system you use to file your resources.

_____

_____

Enlisting Volunteers

Mrs. Oops went out of her way to recruit volunteers for her classroom. She was delighted when four mothers, three fathers, two grandparents, and six students from a local high school volunteered their services. Unfortunately, once they called her to find out exactly what they were supposed to do, the only answer she could give them was "Just come in any time and help out." As you would expect, her list of volunteers dwindled very quickly.

Please help Miss Oops make a list of jobs that she could assign to different volunteers.

_____

_____

PROGRAM MANAGEMENT • *Observation Opportunity*

Name _____

Attend a staff meeting at an early childhood center, or attend a meeting of a professional organization. Submit the agenda of the meeting, and then describe three issues or items that were discussed at it.

Location of the meeting: _____

Date: _____   **Time:** _____

1. _____
   _____
   _____
   _____

2. _____
   _____
   _____
   _____

3. _____
   _____
   _____
   _____

General observations:

_____
_____
_____
_____
_____

PROGRAM MANAGEMENT • Challenge Activities

Name _____

Challenge 1

Create a teacher-made material/toy for your setting that is designed to enhance a particular skill. Use it with children, and then complete the following worksheet.

Name of educational material or toy that you have created:

_____

Age group: _____

Description of item:

_____

_____

Objective: What will the children learn from this?

_____

_____

Materials used to create your educational material/toy:

_____

_____

Procedures: How will this item be presented to the children?

_____

_____

Evaluation: Did the use of the material/toy turn out the way you planned? What changes would you make the next time you use this material/toy?

_____

_____

Challenge 2

Identify five skills and describe an activity that you could use to help a child develop each one.

Skill	Activity
1. _____	_____
_____	_____
_____	_____
_____	_____
2. _____	_____
_____	_____
_____	_____
_____	_____
3. _____	_____
_____	_____
_____	_____
_____	_____
4. _____	_____
_____	_____
_____	_____
_____	_____
5. _____	_____
_____	_____
_____	_____
_____	_____

PROGRAM MANAGEMENT • Post-Training Wrap-Up

After completing this unit, review your personal goal and action plan and describe how you accomplished your goal.

_____

_____

_____

_____

List at least three ways in which you changed your behavior as a result of your training in this Functional Area.

1. _____

2. _____

3. _____

PROGRAM MANAGEMENT • Professional Resource File

Resource Items

Collect the items for the Professional Resource File related to this Functional Area (if applicable). Refer to the pages at the back of this *Trainee's Manual* (pp. 281–283) and to the CDA booklet from the Council for Professional Recognition for specific instructions.

Statement of Competence

Write an essay of 200 to 500 words, listing one or more goals for yourself and for the children and families in the area of Program Management and describing activities you do to achieve these goals. Describe your experiences in your own words. Be concise. Use "I" statements—for example, "I meet with my co-teachers at least once a week to plan our activities and to discuss any issues that might have come up with individual children."

For additional information about writing your Statement of Competence, refer to the workbook section at the end of this *Trainee's Manual* (pp. 283–312) and to the CDA booklet from the Council for Professional Recognition.

Competency Goal VI

To maintain a commitment to professionalism

Chapter 13

Professionalism

Overview

A *professional* is defined in the *American Heritage Dictionary of English Language* as "one who has an assured competence in a particular field or occupation." The professional early childhood teacher/caregiver has a strong knowledge of early childhood theories and effective practices. This ever-growing knowledge base informs her judgment and guides her daily activities.

Rationale

Because children's developmental course is determined in large part by their early experiences, caregivers and teachers of young children play a critical role in shaping the future of our country. Recognizing the importance of our professional role, we must not only follow the best practices and maintain the highest ethics of the profession, but we must also continually strive to increase and share our own knowledge and serve as advocates for children.

Objectives

● **Objective 1**   To seek opportunities to increase professional knowledge and improve professional skills

● **Objective 2**   To serve as an advocate for children and families

● **Objective 3**   To maintain the ethics of the early childhood profession

● **Objective 4**   To build a professional support system

PROFESSIONALISM • Pretest

Complete each of the following items as indicated.

1. List two characteristics of a professional.

   a. _____

   b. _____

2. A teacher was very concerned about public policy relating to children. She wanted all the parents of the children in her class to become child advocates. Put an "X" in front of each thing she did that was appropriate.

   _____ a. Informed parents of a television special devoted to children's issues

   _____ b. Invited a candidate for the state senate who was pro-children to speak at a parent's meeting

   _____ c. Sent a notice home to parents reminding them to vote on election day

   _____ d. Upon the request of the director, invited the candidates who were running for local office

   _____ e. Wrote a column for the parents newsletter discussing four issues related to children

3. List three places in your area where you could go for courses or workshops to learn more about early childhood care and education.

   a. _____

   b. _____

   c. _____

PROFESSIONALISM • Self-Assessment

Indicate how you feel about your skills and abilities in each of the following categories by checking the appropriate column.

	Pretraining		
	Strong	Satisfactory	Needs Improvement
I seek opportunities to increase my professional knowledge and improve my professional skills.	☐	☐	☐
I serve as an advocate for children and families.	☐	☐	☐
I maintain the ethics of the early childhood profession.	☐	☐	☐
I can build a professional support system.	☐	☐	☐

PROFESSIONALISM • Pretraining Personal Goal

Based on your pretraining self-assessment, write a personal goal for this Functional Area and an action plan describing how you will accomplish the goal.

Goal _____

_____

_____

_____

Action Plan _____

_____

_____

_____

_____

_____

_____

_____

_____

_____

_____

_____

Save your goal and action plan for the end of this unit so you will be able to answer these questions: How did you accomplish your goal? And how has your behavior changed based on your training?

To seek opportunities to increase professional knowledge and improve professional skills

Gina had just graduated from high school and was looking through the "Help Wanted" ads. She was debating between applying for two jobs and made a list of the pros and cons for each job.

Waitress	**Infant Caregiver**
Pros:	*Pros:*
Good pay	Babies are cute
Cute uniform	No work at night
May meet a guy	Easy work, you don't need to know anything
Cons:	*Cons:*
Some people are rude	Bad pay
Late nights	Babies sometimes smell bad
Hard work	Have to get up early

When Gina's mother looked at the list, she told her daughter not to bother applying for a job in child care. Gina's mother was right. Child care is not something that you do after school just to make money or fill your time. Caring for young children requires knowledge, dedication, and a willingness to work. It is a profession with an established body of knowledge that is continually expanding. When we accept a job in child care, we are entering a noble profession that can become a lifelong career.

Help Gina's mother. List three reasons Gina should not consider going into child care.

1. _____

   _____

2. _____

   _____

3. _____

   _____

To serve as an advocate for children and families

Miss Hammerhead was conducting her weekly staff meeting. At the end of the formal agenda, Miss Hammerhead shared with her staff some issues related to children that would be debated at the next state legislative session. She felt these three issues were of particular concern:

1. The importance of passing a revision to the child care licensing law to reduce the number of 2-year-old children allowed per adult

2. The importance of passing a law requiring that children under 4 be placed in an approved car seat

3. The importance of finding money in the state budget that would support resource and referral programs, substantially reduce the number of children wait-listed for subsidized child care, and provide scholarships with stipends for child care givers who are seeking professional certificates and degrees

Miss Hammerhead suggested that the staff at the center should keep up with children's issues and should visit or write their legislators, urging them to support legislation that fosters the well-being of children and their families.

Before Miss Hammerhead could finish her discussion, Miss Knucklehead stood up and said, "This is a free country. I don't think you have any right to mix up child care and politics. I'm going to support any issue I want to, and I don't like to be told what to do, or how to vote, or what people I should go and visit."

Miss Hammerhead needs your help. List three important points Miss Hammerhead could make in response to Miss Knucklehead's attack.

1. _____

_____

2. _____

_____

3. _____

_____

To maintain the ethics of the early childhood profession

Maintaining professional ethics is an essential attribute of all child care workers. In responding to children, parents, and co-workers, caregivers make many decisions every day that reflect values and require sensitive judgment. Conducting oneself in an ethical and professional manner involves the following:

- Keeping the best interests of children in mind at all times
- Abiding by the child care regulations of your county and your state
- Maintaining your personal honesty and integrity in all situations
- Treating all children and adults with care and respect regardless of age, gender, and race/ethnic background
- Maintaining confidentiality
- Reporting suspected child abuse and neglect in accordance with your state legislation

In most situations, maintaining professional ethics is a straightforward decision. It is easy to recognize the appropriate ethical behavior when a parent asks for information about another parent or when a fellow worker treats a child in a way that is damaging. However, many situations involving ethical decision making require making a judgment call.

Miss Right-O was holding a regularly scheduled conference with Dorothea's mother, Mrs. My-Way. Miss Right-O talked about some of the activities Dorothea enjoyed and some concerns she had about Dorothea. Dorothea was difficult to engage in an activity and was often disruptive in class. Mrs. My-Way explained that Dorothea was a really good kid at home, except when she was influenced by some older friends. She knew that Dorothea was always talking about a neat kid at the center, Alexander. Dorothea's mother had a strong feeling that Dorothea was imitating the behavior of this new friend. She asked the teacher, Miss Right-O, to describe Alexander. "What neighborhood does he live in? What kind of work do his parents do? Is he disruptive in class? Does he have problems at home?"

Choose the response that you feel would be most appropriate for the teacher, Miss Right-O, to give to the parent, Mrs. My-Way.

_____ *Response 1:* "I would like to discuss Alexander and his family with you, but it's against our code of ethics to disclose information."

_____ *Response 2:* "The problem is Alexander, *not* Dorothea. You'll have to take my word for it."

_____ *Response 3:* "I can't tell you too much about Alexander because I'm not supposed to. But you are right; he doesn't have a good home life."

_____ *Response 4:* "I understand your concern about Dorothea's selection of playmates. However, I feel that your goal and my goal is to help Dorothea learn acceptable behavior, regardless of who she is playing with. What have you found that is most effective?"

To build a professional support system

When we ask caregivers why they choose to work in child care, the typical response is "Because I love children." While a love of children is what draws so many caregivers into the profession, being a caregiver can also be a lonesome experience. After spending hours with young children—serving as leader, decision maker, and problem solver—caregivers quite naturally feel a strong need to share their experiences and discuss their concerns with other caregivers within or outside their workplace. Because most caregiving jobs require caregivers to spend a full day with their children, finding time to be with colleagues is not always easy.

Making time for caregivers to meet together, plan together, and share ideas is in large part the responsibility of the center director. When planning and sharing time is not built into their working hours, it is up to the caregivers to help the center director realize the benefits to the center that can result from the development of collegial relationships.

Miss Get-Down-to-Work, the director of We're All About Kids child care center, has provided a schedule for each caregiver that allows no time for the staff to get together. She prides herself on the fact that caregivers who work for her never waste their time talking to each other.

Mrs. Let-Your-Hair-Down decided that the time had come to make some changes. She invited her co-workers to a potluck dinner at her house. After dinner, she remarked to her guests that this was the first time they had had a chance to get to know each other. "You know," piped up Miss Speak-Your-Mind, "it's not that I don't like being with kids, but after awhile, I begin to feel like a castaway with not a soul I can talk to."

By the end of the evening, the caregivers had decided on a plan. They would find a way to convince Miss Get-Down-to-Work that they could all do a much better job with the kids if they had some planning and sharing time together as part of their weekly schedule.

List three good arguments that they could present to Miss Get-Down-to-Work that would convince her to revamp their schedules.

1. _____

_____

2. _____

_____

3. _____

_____

Now it's time for the caregivers to decide what else they can do besides talking to the director to make sure that they have time to spend together. What do you suggest?

1. _____

_____

2. _____

_____

3. _____

_____

PROFESSIONALISM • *Observation Opportunity*

Name _____

Identify an issue related to your center that you are concerned about. For example, you feel that the outdoor schedule should be changed, that more equipment is needed in the classroom, or that parents are picking up their children late. Make an appointment with your director to discuss the issue you select.

Issue:

_____

_____

Major points discussed in the interview:

_____

_____

_____

_____

_____

Response of the director:

_____

_____

_____

_____

Follow-up actions:

_____

_____

_____

_____

PROFESSIONALISM • Challenge Activities

Name _____

Challenge 1

Complete the following chart by identifying the opportunities available to you that will enhance your professional growth.

Professional Conferences/ Courses/Workshops	Presentations Offered	Location
1. _____	_____	_____
2. _____	_____	_____
3. _____	_____	_____

Professional Journals	Article Subject or Title	Author
1. _____	_____	_____
2. _____	_____	_____

Early Childhood Websites	Web Address	Subject
1. _____	_____	_____
2. _____	_____	_____

Professional Books	Subject	Author
1. _____	_____	_____
2. _____	_____	_____

Challenge 2

Think of an issue in the field of early childhood that is important to you. Write a letter about this issue to someone of importance from your area, county, or state, such as a school board member, council member, senator, representative, or member of an early childhood advisory board. Or write a letter to the editor of a local newspaper. Explain your issue and why you want to bring it to this person's attention.

_____

_____

_____

_____

_____

_____

_____

_____

_____

_____

_____

_____

_____

_____

_____

_____

_____

_____

_____

PROFESSIONALISM • Post-Training Wrap-Up

After completing this unit, review your personal goal and action plan and describe how you accomplished your goal.

_____

_____

_____

_____

List at least three ways in which you changed your behavior as a result of your training in this Functional Area.

1. _____

2. _____

3. _____

PROFESSIONALISM • Professional Resource File

Resource Items

Collect the items for the Professional Resource File related to this Functional Area (if applicable). Refer to the pages at the back of this *Trainee's Manual* (pp. 281–283) and to the CDA booklet from the Council for Professional Recognition for specific instructions

Statement of Competence

Write an essay of 200 to 500 words, listing one or more goals for yourself and for the children and families in the area of Professionalism and describing activities you do to achieve these goals. Describe your experiences in your own words. Be concise. Use "I" statements—for example, "I decided to complete my CDA in order to improve my ability to work with young children and families and to advance my career. I frequently read articles in *PreK Today* to get new ideas to use with my group of children."

For additional information about writing your Statement of Competence, refer to the workbook section at the end of this *Trainee's Manual* (pp. 283–312) and to the CDA booklet from the Council for Professional Recognition.

Preparing the CDA Professional Resource File

The *Professional Resource File* is a collection of materials that demonstrate your ability to meet the Competency Goals described in the *Child Development Associate (CDA) Assessment System and Competency Standards* booklet. The Resource File is part of the national CDA assessment system of the Council for Professional Recognition. It includes three sections:

1. Autobiography
2. Resource Collection
3. Statements of Competence

Format

The Council does not specify a required format for the Professional Resource File. However, CDA candidates have found the following systems to work well:

- A 3" three-ring binder with plastic pages
- An accordion-style file box with a handle
- A plastic office file box with a handle and hanging file folders

Using labeled tab dividers, file folders, and/or file labels will keep your Resource File organized, professional looking, and easy to access.

While you may want to include many additional resources in your Resource File, for the national CDA assessment, the items that are specifically required must be clearly identified.

1. Autobiography Create a 300-word statement telling a few things about yourself and describing what led you to work with young children. To write your autobiography, respond to the following questions or prompts:

  a. Briefly describe your childhood, where you were born and raised, and your family today.

  b. What education have you completed?

  c. Describe any memorable events in your life.

  d. What things do you enjoy doing in your spare time?

  e. What events led you to work with young children?

2. Resource Collection The CDA Council for Professional Recognition specifies resources to collect in preparation for the national CDA credentialing assessment. Refer to the section on Resource Collection that follows and to the CDA booklet for complete descriptions of the designated resource items.

3. Statements of Competence The Professional Resource File includes short essays of 200 to 500 words, reflecting your work with children, for each of the following Competency Goals:

  Goal I: To establish and maintain a safe, healthy learning environment
  Functional Areas: Safe, Healthy, and Learning Environment

  Goal II: To advance physical and intellectual competence
  Functional Areas: Physical, Cognitive, Communication, and Creative

  Goal III: To support social and emotional development and provide positive guidance
  Functional Areas: Self, Social, and Guidance

  Goal IV: To establish positive and productive relationships with families
  Functional Area: Families

  Goal V: To ensure a well-run, purposeful program responsive to participant needs
  Functional Area: Program Management

  Goal VI: To maintain a commitment to professionalism
  Functional Area: Professionalism

Resource Collection*

For Competency Goal I:

1. Provide a summary of the legal requirements in your state regarding child abuse and neglect (including contact information for the appropriate agency) and also your program's policy regarding your responsibility to report child abuse and neglect.

2. Include the current certificate of completion of a certified pediatric first aid training course (that includes treatment for blocked airway and providing rescue breathing for infants and young children). Certification must have been within the past three years.

3. Use the Internet, public library, or your program's professional library to obtain the name and contact information for an agency that supplies information on nutrition for children and/or nutrition education for families (e.g., cooperative extension service or child care food program).

4. Provide a sample of your weekly plan that includes goals for children's learning and development, brief descriptions of planned learning experiences, and also accommodations for special needs (whether for children you currently serve or may serve in the future).

For Competency Goal II:

5. Select four songs, finger plays, word games, or poems that you can use to promote phonological awareness. Describe strategies to promote phonological awareness among children whose home language is other than English.

6. *For preschool endorsement:* Describe nine learning experiences for 3-, 4-, and 5-year-old children—three for 3-year-olds, three for 4-year-olds, and three for 5-year-olds. Each learning experience should promote physical, cognitive, and creative development. Describe the goals, materials, and teaching strategies used.

   For infant/toddler endorsement: Describe nine learning experiences that promote physical, cognitive, and creative development—three for young infants, three for mobile infants, and three for toddlers. Describe the goals, materials, and teaching strategies used.

   For family child care endorsement: Describe nine learning experiences that promote physical, cognitive, and creative development—three for infants, three for toddlers, and three for preschoolers. Describe the goals, materials, and teaching strategies used.

*Based on Brunson Day, C. (Ed.). (2004). *Essentials for Child Development Associates* (2nd ed.). Washington, DC: Council for Professional Development.

For Competency Goal III:

7. Provide the titles, authors, publishers, copyright dates, and short summaries of ten age-appropriate children's books that you use to support the development of children's self-concept and self-esteem and to help children deal with life's challenges. These books may support development of cultural and linguistic group identity; gender identity; children with disabilities or special needs; separation, divorce, remarriage, or blended families; everyday activities and routines; and/or the cycle of life, from human reproduction to death.

8. Use the Internet, public library, or your program's professional library to obtain at least two resources designed to assist teachers in constructively dealing with children with challenging behaviors (for instance, aggressive behavior, such as hitting or biting, or shyness).

9. Provide the name and telephone number of an agency in the community where you work for making referrals to family counseling.

For Competency Goal IV:

10. Find out where to obtain resources, materials, and translation services for families whose home language is other than English. Provide the agency name and contact information.

11. Document your program's policies that specify parents' responsibilities and what the program does for parents.

For Competency Goal V:

12. Provide three samples of record-keeping forms used in early childhood programs. Include an accident report, an emergency form, and a third form of your choice.

For Competency Goal VI:

13. Use the Internet, public library, or your program's professional library to obtain the name, address, and phone number of your state's agency that regulates child care centers and homes. These regulations are available electronically at the website of the National Resource Center for Health and Safety in Child Care (http://nrc.uchsc.edu/STATES/states.htm). Make a copy of the section(s) that describes qualification requirements for personnel (teachers, directors, and assistants).

    For family child care: If your state does not regulate family child care homes, review the accreditation standards of the National Association for Family Child Care. Describe two important requirements related to your job responsibilities.

14. Review the websites of two or three national early childhood associations (one with a local affiliate) to obtain information about membership, resources, and how to order (if necessary, use the public library for Internet access). Download and include at least two resources from the Internet that will enhance your work.

15. Obtain four pamphlets or articles (may be downloaded from the Internet) designed to help parents understand how young children develop and learn.

    For preschool endorsement: The articles must help parents understand the development and learning of 3- to 5-year-olds. At least one article must relate to guidance.

    For infant/toddler endorsement: The articles must help parents understand how babies and toddlers (birth to age 3) develop and learn. At least one article must relate to brain development.

    For family child care endorsement: The articles must help parents understand the development and learning of children birth to age 5. At least one article must relate to guidance.

16. Locate an observation tool to use in recording information about children's behavior. One copy should be blank; the other should be filled out as a sample of your observation of an individual child. (*The child's name should not be included.*)

17. Obtain contact information for at least two agencies in the community that provide resources and services for children with disabilities. (In most communities, the local school district provides these services.)

Writing the Statements of Competence

Completing the following worksheets will provide a method for stimulating ideas and organizing your thoughts in order to write your Statements of Competence.

Throughout the course, the Challenges section in each Functional Area of the *Trainee's Manual* directs you to write the related statement.

Each Statement of Competence includes the goals you have for children and families and specific examples of activities you should do to achieve those goals.

Not all of the ideas you come up with doing the worksheets can be included in your statements, since the national CDA limits each statement to 200 to 500 words.

Competency Goal I To establish and maintain a safe, healthy learning environment

Make a cover page with this Competency Goal Statement.

Functional Areas: Safe, Healthy, Learning Environment

Safe

Write a statement that explains how you keep the environment safe for the children in your care. Give examples that describe what you do.

This statement needs to be 75 to 150 words. The statements for the Functional Areas of Safe, Healthy, and Learning Environment together need to be 200 to 500 words.

Note: Candidates applying for the national CDA with an infant/toddler endorsement need to give examples in all three age groups: young infants (0–8 months), mobile infants (8–17 months), and toddlers (17–36 months). With rapidly developing motor skills come new challenges of keeping the children safe. Describe the unique developmental concerns for each age group.

Review the information on Safe from the textbook, *Trainee's Manual,* and handouts distributed in class. Refer to the activities completed in class.

Step 1: Introduction

Begin your statement with the goal provided by the Council for Professional Recognition:

> **Functional Area 1: Safe.** *Candidate provides a safe environment to prevent and reduce injuries.*

Step 2: Goals

State your own goals for the Functional Area of Safe:

_____

_____

Step 3: Activities to Achieve Your Goals

a. Give some examples of how you keep the indoor and outdoor environments safe and how you prevent accidents from occurring. For example, remember that supervision is the most important way to prevent accidents and reduce injuries.

   _____

   _____

   _____

   _____

b. Describe systems or checks you have in place at the center to be sure that the environment is safe. For example, how do you keep children from getting into unsafe items? What fire drills do you help conduct? Describe the locations of your fire evacuation diagram, first aid kit, and emergency phone numbers.

   _____

   _____

   _____

c. Describe the first aid or CPR certifications that you hold.

   _____

   _____

d. Give examples of the activities that you do with children to teach them and their families about being safe—for example, fire safety, stranger danger, safety crossing streets, safety on play equipment, car seat safety checks, providing resources for parents.

   _____

   _____

e. Describe how you model appropriate behavior for the children.

   _____

   _____

Based on these ideas, write your Statement of Competence for Safe.

Healthy

Write a statement that explains how you keep the children in your care healthy. Give examples that describe what you do.

This statement needs to be 75 to 150 words. The statements for the Functional Areas of Safe, Healthy, and Learning Environment together need to be 200 to 500 words.

Note: Candidates applying for the national CDA with an infant/toddler endorsement need to give examples in all three age groups: young infants (0–8 months), mobile infants (8–17 months), and toddlers (17–36 months). The infant's day is centered on meeting her individual needs, while the toddler is starting to learn new health habits that include eating nutritiously, handwashing, and understanding toileting.

Review the information on Healthy from the textbook, *Trainee's Manual*, and handouts distributed in class. Refer to the activities completed in class.

Step 1: Introduction

Begin your statement with the goal provided by the Council for Professional Recognition:

> **Functional Area 2: Healthy.** *Candidate promotes good health and nutrition and provides an environment that contributes to the prevention of illness.*

Step 2: Goals

State your own goals for the Functional Area of Healthy:

_____

_____

Step 3: Activities to Achieve Your Goals

a. Describe some of the ways you keep the children healthy through classroom practices:

- Handwashing—when and how, for children and adults (required item!)
- Disinfecting of room and materials
- Toothbrushing
- Serving nutritious snacks and meals
- Providing rest time for children
- Promoting physical activity

- Practicing universal precautions
- Ensuring immunizations and physicals are kept up to date
- Placing infants on their backs when they sleep

_____

_____

_____

_____

b. Describe what you do when children are not well, how you administer medication, or how you exchange information with families about children's physical health.

_____

_____

_____

c. Explain your knowledge of the signs and symptoms of child abuse and neglect and how to report it.

_____

_____

_____

d. Give some examples of the activities that you do with the children to teach them about health. Some items to consider:
- Cooking nutritious snacks
- Covering our mouths when we sneeze and cough
- Dramatic play of doctor, dentist, restaurant, and so on
- Brushing teeth; a dentist visiting to talk to the children
- Using the toilet

_____

_____

_____

_____

e. Give examples of how you exchange information with families about children's health, including placing resources for parents on the parent board or sending home a daily note to parents regarding health-related issues.

_____

_____

_____

_____

Based on these ideas, write your Statement of Competence for Healthy.

Learning Environment

Write a statement that explains how you set up the room, what kinds of materials you have in the room, and the schedule you follow. Give examples that describe what you do.

This statement needs to be 75 to 150 words. This statement goes along with those for Safe and Healthy for the completion of Competency Goal I. The statements for the Functional Areas of Safe, Healthy, and Learning Environment together need to be 200 to 500 words.

Note: Candidates applying for the national CDA with an infant/toddler endorsement need to give examples in all three age groups: young infants (0–8 months), mobile infants (8–17 months), and toddlers (17–36 months). Describe some of the areas and materials you would have for each age group.

Review the information on Learning Environment from the textbook, *Trainee's Manual,* and handouts distributed in class. Refer to the activities completed in class.

Step 1: Introduction

Begin your statement with the goal provided by the Council for Professional Recognition:

> **Functional Area 3: Learning Environment.** *Candidate uses space, relationships, materials, and routines as resources for constructing an interesting, secure, and enjoyable environment that encourages play, exploration, and learning.*

Step 2: Goals

State your own goals for the Functional Area of Learning Environment:

_____

_____

Step 3: Activities to Achieve Your Goals

a. Describe the centers in your room—for example, Infants—play, feeding, changing, sleeping, parent; Toddler—library, dramatic play, manipulatives, indoor large muscle, changing; Preschool—library, dramatic play, blocks, art, manipulatives.

_____

_____

_____

_____

b. Describe the layout of your room. How does your room arrangement encourage play, allow for exploration, and provide convenience—for example, clearly defined areas so children can focus on their activities, art activities near the sink, active centers located near one another, diaper and food preparation areas separated, spaces where active mobile infants will not harm younger infants, and so on?

_____

_____

_____

_____

c. Describe some of the other features in your room—for example, cultural diversity, artwork displayed at the children's level, shelves labeled to promote independence in the children, and the like.

_____

_____

_____

_____

d. Describe how your daily schedule meets the needs of the children—for example, most of the children's time is spent in self-directed play; meals, diapering/toileting, and napping are appropriate for the age group; there is a balance of active and quiet play; there is daily outdoor time; infants and toddlers have individual schedules; the schedule is flexible. (Don't include the actual schedule, just a brief description.)

_____

_____

_____

_____

Based on these ideas, write your Statement of Competence for Learning Environment.

Combine your statements for Safe, Healthy, and Learning Environment to make up your Statement of Competence (200 to 500 words) for Competency Goal I.

Competency Goal II   To advance physical and intellectual competence

Make a cover page with this Competency Goal Statement.

Functional Areas: Physical, Cognitive, Communication, Creative

Physical

Write a statement that explains how you provide activities to promote the physical development of children in your care. Give examples that describe what you do.

This statement needs to be 75 to 150 words. The statements for the Functional Areas of Physical, Cognitive, Communication, and Creative together need to be 200 to 500 words.

Note: Candidates applying for the national CDA with an infant/toddler endorsement need to give examples in all three age groups: young infants (0–8 months), mobile infants (8–17 months), and toddlers (17–36 months). Briefly describe some of the items and activities you provide that promote physical development of the children at different ages.

Review the information on Physical from the textbook, *Trainee's Manual*, and handouts distributed in class. Refer to the activities completed in class.

Step 1: Introduction

Begin your statement with the goal provided by the Council for Professional Recognition:

> **Functional Area 4: Physical.** *Candidate provides a variety of equipment, activities, and opportunities to promote the physical development of children.*

Step 2: Goals

State your own goals for the Functional Area of Physical:

_____

_____

Step 3: Activities to Achieve Your Goals

a. Describe how your schedule provides time for activities that promote both small- and large-muscle development (indoors and outdoors).

_____

_____

_____

b. Describe the types of large-muscle activities and materials/equipment that you provide.

_____

_____

_____

c. Describe the types of small-muscle activities and materials/equipment that you provide.

_____

_____

_____

d. Describe ways that you participate with children in physical activities.

_____

_____

_____

_____

e. Describe ways that you provide opportunities for children to develop
their senses—sight, smell, touch, hearing, and tasting.

_____

_____

_____

_____

_____

_____

Based on these ideas, write your Statement of Competence for Physical.

Cognitive

Write a statement that explains how you arrange the environment, provide
appropriate activities/materials, and offer encouragement to promote the
cognitive development of the children in your care. Give examples that
describe what you do.

This statement needs to be 75 to 150 words. The statements for the
Functional Areas of Physical, Cognitive, Communication, and Creative
together need to be 200 to 500 words.

Note: Candidates applying for the national CDA with an infant/toddler
endorsement need to give examples for all three age groups: young infants
(0–8 months), mobile infants (8–17 months), and toddlers (17–36 months).
Briefly describe some of the items and activities that are age appropriate
for each group.

Review the information on Cognitive from the textbook, *Trainee's Manual,*
and handouts distributed in class. Refer to the activities completed in class.

Step 1: Introduction

Begin your statement with the goal provided by the Council for Professional Recognition:

> **Functional Area 5: Cognitive.** *Candidate provides activities and opportunities that encourage curiosity, exploration, and problem solving appropriate to the development levels and learning styles of children.*

Step 2: Goals

State your own goals for the Functional Area of Cognitive:

_____

_____

Step 3: Activities to Achieve Your Goals

a. Describe ways in which the environment, schedule, materials, and activities promote exploration—for example, open shelving so materials are accessible to children, ample time planned for activities and for thinking, emphasis on center or free play time, and the like.

_____

_____

_____

b. Describe the types of activities and materials/equipment that you provide for cognitive development.

_____

_____

_____

_____

_____

_____

_____

_____

c. Describe your interactions with the children that encourage their cognitive development—for example, join children in play, use questioning to further their thinking, understand that children learn through repetition of the familiar, provide encouraging words, and so on.

_____

_____

_____

_____

_____

_____

d. Describe how you observe children so that you can provide the appropriate materials and activities to meet their individual needs.

_____

_____

_____

e. List special materials you have made to promote cognitive development.

_____

_____

_____

_____

_____

_____

_____

Based on these ideas, write your Statement of Competence for Cognitive.

Communication

Write a statement that explains how you help children communicate. Give examples that describe how you help children understand and use verbal and nonverbal means of communicating thoughts and feelings.

This statement needs to be 75 to 150 words. The statements for the Functional Areas of Physical, Cognitive, Communication, and Creative together need to be 200 to 500 words.

Note: Candidates applying for the national CDA with an infant/toddler endorsement need to give examples for all three age groups: young infants (0–8 months), mobile infants (8–17 months), and toddlers (17–36 months). Describe how you are attentive to the verbal and nonverbal needs of children of different ages.

Review the information on Communication from the textbook, *Trainee's Manual,* and handouts distributed in class. Refer to the activities completed in class.

Step 1: Introduction

Begin your statement with the goal provided by the Council for Professional Recognition:

> **Functional Area 6: Communication.** *Candidate actively communicates with children and provides opportunities and support for children to understand, acquire, and use verbal and nonverbal means of communicating thoughts and feelings.*

Step 2: Goals

State your own goals for the Functional Area of Communication:

_____

_____

Step 3: Activities to Achieve Your Goals

a. Describe ways you talk with children on a regular and individual basis.

_____

_____

_____

b. List the types of activities and materials/equipment that you provide for language development—for example, books, songs, finger plays, and so on.

_____

_____

_____

_____

c. Describe your interactions with children that encourage communication—for example, have conversations with the children, listen closely when children talk, use questioning to further their understanding, provide encouraging words, and so on.

_____

_____

_____

_____

_____

d. Describe how you observe the children so you can provide appropriate materials and activities or so you can refer children who may need to be evaluated for speech and/or language intervention.

_____

_____

_____

_____

e. Describe special materials you have made to promote language development.

_____

_____

_____

_____

f. Describe how you support children and families in your program who speak other languages.

_____

_____

_____

_____

_____

Based on these ideas, write your Statement of Competence for Communication.

Creative

Write a statement that explains how you support children's creativity. Give examples that describe what you do.

This statement needs to be 75 to 150 words. The statements for the Functional Areas of Physical, Cognitive, Communication, and Creative together need to be 200 to 500 words.

Note: Candidates applying for the national CDA with an infant/toddler endorsement need to give examples for all three age groups: young infants (0–8 months), mobile infants (8–17 months), and toddlers (17–36 months). Infants can be creative in the ways they interact with their world. Toddlers are starting to enjoy creative expression.

Review the information on Creative from the textbook, *Trainee's Manual,* and handouts distributed in class. Refer to the activities completed in class.

Step 1: Introduction

Begin your statement with the goal provided by the Council for Professional Recognition:

> **Functional Area 7: Creative.** *Candidate provides opportunities that stimulate children to play with sound, rhythm, language, materials, space, and ideas in individual ways and to express their creative abilities.*

Step 2: Goals

State your own goals for the Functional Area of Creative:

_____

_____

Step 3: Activities to Achieve Your Goals

a. Describe your philosophy about children and creativity (process versus product, individual expression).

_____

_____

_____

b. Describe the types of activities and materials/equipment that you provide for creativity. (Include more than just art experiences.)

_____

_____

_____

_____

_____

_____

c. Describe how you allow time and space for children to be creative—for example, providing ready access to materials, encouraging sensory and messy play, and the like.

_____

_____

_____

_____

_____

_____

d. Describe your interactions with children that encourage their creativity—for example, participate in children's play, encourage them to try new things, add new and different items, allow unconventional use of materials, and so forth.

_____

_____

_____

_____

_____

_____

_____

e. Describe any special cultural items you provide for the children (music, cooking, dramatic play).

_____

_____

_____

_____

_____

f. Describe how are you able to show your creativity as a teacher.

_____

_____

_____

_____

_____

Based on these ideas, write your Statement of Competence for Creative.

Combine your statements for Physical, Cognitive, Communication, and Creative to make up your Statement of Competence (200 to 500 words) for Competency Goal II.

Competency Goal III To support social and emotional development and provide positive guidance

Make a cover page with this Competency Goal Statement.

Functional Areas: Self, Social, Guidance

Self

Write a statement that explains how you support each child's sense of self. Give examples that describe what you do.

This statement needs to be 75 to 150 words. The statements for the Functional Areas of Self, Social, and Guidance together need to be 200 to 500 words.

Note: Candidates applying for the national CDA with an infant/toddler endorsement need to give examples for all three age groups: young infants (0–8 months), mobile infants (8–17 months), and toddlers (17–36 months). Infants are learning to build a sense of trust, and toddlers are starting to develop independence.

Review the information on Self from the textbook, *Trainee's Manual,* and handouts distributed in class. Refer to the activities completed in class.

Step 1: Introduction

Begin your statement with the goal provided by the Council for Professional Recognition:

> **Functional Area 8: Self.** *Candidate provides physical and emotional security for each child and helps each child to know, accept, and take pride in himself or herself and to develop a sense of independence.*

Step 2: Goals

State your own goals for the Functional Area of Self:

_____

_____

Step 3: Activities to Achieve Your Goals

a. Describe how you provide an emotionally safe and secure environment for the children. (Include how you involve families in this process.)

_____

_____

b. Describe how you help children recognize and handle their feelings and
    deal with difficult situations.

_____

_____

_____

_____

c. Describe how you show affection to children and help them feel loved.

_____

_____

_____

_____

d. Describe how you help children develop a sense of personal identity,
    feelings of self-worth, and a sense of their own family and culture.

_____

_____

_____

_____

_____

e. Describe how you help young children increase their self-help skills, such
    as eating, toileting, getting dressed, and cleaning up.

_____

_____

_____

_____

_____

_____

Based on these ideas, write your Statement of Competence for Self.

Social

Write a statement that explains how you support children's development of social skills. Give examples that describe what you do.

This statement needs to be 75 to 150 words. The statements for the Functional Areas of Self, Social, and Guidance together need to be 200 to 500 words.

Note: Candidates applying for the national CDA with an infant/toddler endorsement need to give examples for all three age groups: young infants (0–8 months), mobile infants (8–17 months), and toddlers (17–36 months). Briefly describe some of the activities/items you provide to promote social skills for children of different age groups. Remember that an infant's primary interactions are with the adults who care for him.

Review the information on Social from the textbook, *Trainee's Manual*, and handouts distributed in class. Refer to the activities completed in class.

Step 1: Introduction

Begin your statement with the goal provided by the Council for Professional Recognition:

> **Functional Area 9: Social.** *Candidate helps each child feel accepted in the group, helps children learn to communicate and get along with others, and encourages feelings of empathy and mutual respect among children and adults.*

Step 2: Goals

State your own goals for the Functional Area of Social:

_____

_____

Step 3: Activities to Achieve Your Goals

a. List the types of activities and materials/equipment you provide to promote social skills, cooperation, and friend-making behavior—for example, group games and projects where children work together.

_____

_____

_____

_____

b. Describe how your center allows for time (schedule) and space (environment) for children to learn how to develop social skills through interact-
ing with one another—for example, providing time in activity areas where
children select their playmates.

_____

_____

_____

_____

_____

_____

c. Describe how you promote prosocial behavior and help children get
along together in your classroom.

_____

_____

_____

_____

_____

_____

d. Describe your interactions with children that encourage their social
skills—for example, you participate in the children's play, model social
behaviors with the children and with other adults, and so on.

_____

_____

_____

_____

_____

_____

Based on these ideas, write your Statement of Competence for Social.

Guidance

Write a statement that explains how you provide positive guidance and help children learn appropriate behaviors. Give examples that describe what you do.

This statement needs to be 75 to 150 words. The statements for the Functional Areas of Self, Social, and Guidance together need to be 200 to 500 words.

Note: Candidates applying for the national CDA with an infant/toddler endorsement need to give examples for all three age groups: young infants (0–8 months), mobile infants (8–17 months), and toddlers (17–36 months). Remember that setting up the environment and providing supervision are the most appropriate ways of guiding the youngest children.

Review the information on Guidance from the textbook, *Trainee's Manual*, and handouts distributed in class. Refer to the activities completed in class.

Step 1: Introduction

Begin your statement with the goal provided by the Council for Professional Recognition:

> **Functional Area 10: Guidance.** *Candidate provides a supportive environment in which children can begin to learn and practice appropriate and acceptable behaviors as individuals and as a group.*

Step 2: Goals

State your own goals for the Functional Area of Guidance:

_____

_____

Step 3: Activities to Achieve Your Goals

a. Describe some of the positive guidance methods you use—for example, giving choices, restating rules, ignoring, using encouraging words, and using positive reinforcement. Give two or three specific examples.

_____

_____

_____

_____

b. Describe how you support children through transitions from one activity to the next.

_____

_____

_____

_____

_____

_____

c. Explain how you help children learn guidelines and limits—for example, rules are stated positively, expectations are clear and consistent, older children help develop class guidelines, and so on.

_____

_____

_____

_____

_____

_____

d. Describe how you record children's behavior for use in working cooperatively with parents or to make referrals for assessment.

_____

_____

_____

_____

_____

_____

Based on these ideas, write your Statement of Competence for Guidance.

Combine your statements for Self, Social, and Guidance to make up your Statement of Competence (200 to 500 words) for Competency Goal III.

Competency Goal IV To establish positive and productive relationships with families

Make a cover page with this Competency Goal Statement.

Functional Area: Families

Families

Write a statement that describes how you maintain an open, friendly, and cooperative relationship with each child's family. Give examples that describe what you do.

This statement needs to be 200 to 500 words. Families is the only Functional Area for this Competency Goal.

Note: Candidates applying for the national CDA with an infant/toddler endorsement need to give examples for all three age groups: young infants (0–8 months), mobile infants (8–17 months), and toddlers (17–36 months). Describe how you work together in establishing individual routines for infants, how you help older infants/toddlers and their parents who may be having difficulty with separating from each other, and how you create an environment that is family friendly.

Review the information on Families from the textbook, *Trainee's Manual*, and handouts distributed in class. Refer to the activities completed in class.

Step 1: Introduction

Begin your statement with the goal provided by the Council for Professional Recognition:

> **Functional Area 11: Families.** *Candidate maintains an open, friendly, and cooperative relationship with each child's family, encourages their involvement in the program, and supports the child's relationship with his or her family.*

Step 2: Goals

State your own goals for the Functional Area of Families:

_____

_____

Step 3: Activities to Achieve Your Goals

a. Describe some of the ways that you communicate or share information with families—for example, newsletters, "What I did today" notes, and bulletin boards. Give at least one specific example.

_____

_____

_____

_____

_____

b. Describe how you help parents understand child growth and development and the importance of play in the learning process.

_____

_____

_____

_____

c. Describe how and when you conduct parent conferences and other ways of meeting with parents.

_____

_____

_____

_____

d. Describe some of the ways you include families in your center's day-to-day and special events. Give specific examples.

_____

_____

_____

_____

e. Describe how you embrace the different cultures of the families that you serve.

_____

_____

_____

_____

f. Explain how you offer support for those families who need information about education, health, social services, or other community resources.

_____

_____

_____

_____

Based on these ideas, write your Statement of Competence for Families.

This Statement of Competence (200 to 500 words) stands alone for Competency Goal IV.

Competency Goal V To ensure a well-run, purposeful program responsive to participant needs

Make a cover page with this Competency Goal Statement.

Functional Area: Program Management

Program Management

Write a statement that explains how you are an effective program manager. Give examples that describe what you do.

This statement needs to be 200 to 500 words. Program Management is the only Functional Area for this Competency Goal.

Review the information on Program Management from the textbook, *Trainee's Manual,* and handouts distributed in class. Refer to the activities completed in class.

Step 1: Introduction

Begin your statement with the goal provided by the Council for Professional Recognition:

> **Functional Area 12: Program Management.** *Candidate is a manager who uses all available resources to ensure an effective operation. The Candidate is a competent organizer, planner, record keeper, communicator, and a cooperative co-worker.*

Step 2: Goals

State your own goals for the Functional Area of Program Management:

_____

_____

Step 3: Activities to Achieve Your Goals

a. Describe the records that you keep for your program (attendance, accident/incident, lesson planning, any regulatory records required).

_____

_____

b. Give examples of how you cooperate with other staff members in your program—for example, having staff meetings, lesson planning, field trip planning, working out playground schedules, and so on.

_____

_____

_____

_____

c. Describe how you observe the children and keep records for meetings with parents (both formal and informal), lesson planning, and program evaluation.

_____

_____

_____

_____

d. Describe any materials that you have made for your classroom or any materials that you have adapted for use by children in your care.

_____

_____

Based on these ideas, write your Statement of Competence for Program Management.

This Statement of Competence (200 to 500 words) stands alone for Competency Goal V.

Competency Goal VI To maintain a commitment to professionalism

Make a cover page with this Competency Goal Statement.

Functional Area: Professionalism

Professionalism

Write a statement that tells how you are a competent, ethical professional. Describe how you work with others and the ways you keep up to date with new information from the field of early childhood. Give examples that describe what you do.

This statement needs to be 200 to 500 words. Professionalism is the only Functional Area for Competency Goal VI.

Review the information on Professionalism from the textbook, *Trainee's Manual*, and handouts distributed in class. Refer to the activities completed in class.

Step 1: Introduction

Begin your statement with the goal provided by the Council for Professional Recognition:

> **Functional Area 13: Professionalism.** *Candidate makes decisions based on knowledge of early childhood theories and practices; Candidate promotes quality in childcare services. Candidate takes advantage of opportunities to improve competence, both for personal and professional growth and for the benefit of children and families.*